This book is a

GIFT

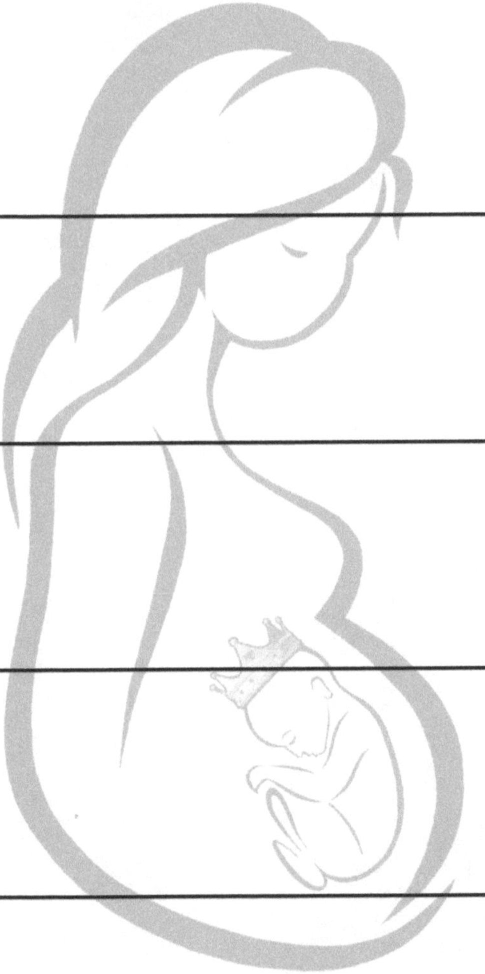

To

____

From

____

Date

____

Note

____

"Blessed is the fruit of your womb".

2

The BLESSEDNESS of BARRENNESS

CHRISTOPHER OGAN

THE BLESSEDNESS OF BARRENNESS

© 2020 Christopher Ogan

Published by **LUMINA Publishing**

ISBN : 978-978-984-221-6

For further information or permission:
Christopher Ogan
Email: contactogan@gmail.com
Tel: +234 810 967 0769
+234 805 618 7774

All scripture quotations are from the King James Version of the Holy Bible unless otherwise stated.

The portions of the scriptures made **bold** are highlighted to emphasis particular areas of interest in the scriptures.

DEDICATION

To all the blessed women who are called barren.

To every couple called to fulfil the call of barrenness.

To all the kingly priests born of the once barren wombs.

CONTENT

ABOUT THIS BOOK

This book is written for those who are presently barren or were once barren. It is also written for the children who are born from the once barren wombs. It will be a blessing to those who are not yet married but who want God to guide them in their choice of a spouse and who would also want to have godly seeds after marriage. It will also be a blessing to those who are married with children and who would want to guide their children in the ways of the LORD and in the fulfilment of their calling.

I must forewarn you however, that this book does not conform to conventional teachings on barrenness and fruitfulness, hence I counsel you to let go of what you have heard or known about barrenness before now and open your heart to the words in this book. If you do this, I can assure you that God will speak to you through the pages of this book.

The revelations about barrenness contained in this book is not given to all and therefore may not be understood by all but those unto whom it is given, will receive, understand and believe it as soon as they read the words in the book. Understanding the revelations in this book is not a product of intelligence, academic attainment or lack of education but rather a product of meekness. Therefore, I pray that you receive with meekness the words written in this book.

The Lord Jesus Christ speaking about barrenness for the first time in His ministry said, all men cannot receive the saying that, **there are people who are created barren by God for the sake of His kingdom,** except those unto whom the word is given.

*Matthew 19:11. But he said unto them, **All men cannot receive this saying, save they to whom it is given.***
*12. For **there are some eunuchs, which were so born from their mother's womb**: and there are some eunuchs, which were made eunuchs of men: and there be eunuchs, which have made themselves eunuchs for the kingdom of heaven's sake. He that is able to receive it, let him receive it.*

The scripture below from prophet Isaiah is a picture of the nature of this book

Isaiah 29:11. And the vision of all is become unto you as the words of a book that is sealed, which men deliver to one that is learned, saying, Read this, I pray thee: and he saith, I cannot; for it is sealed:
12. And the book is delivered to him that is not learned, saying, Read this, I pray thee: and he saith, I am not learned.
17. Is it not yet a very little while, and Lebanon shall be turned into a fruitful field, and the fruitful field shall be esteemed as a forest?
*18. And in that day shall **the deaf hear the words of the book, and the eyes of the blind shall see out of obscurity, and out of darkness.***
*19. **The meek also shall increase their joy in the LORD,** and the poor among men shall rejoice in the Holy One of Israel.*
22. Therefore thus saith the LORD, who redeemed Abraham,

*concerning the house of Jacob, **Jacob shall not now be ashamed,** neither shall his face now wax pale.*

*23. But **when he seeth his children, the work of mine hands, in the midst of him, they shall sanctify my name, and sanctify the Holy One of Jacob**, and shall fear the God of Israel.*

*24. **They also that erred in spirit shall come to understanding,** and they that murmured shall learn doctrine.*

I am glad to let you know that the revelations in this book is written **to deliver the barren from shame** and **for a doctrine** so that those who have erred concerning God's will and purpose concerning barrenness will get to understand the truth, and run with it.

In this book you will see that ***"Barrenness is a natural camouflage over a supernatural agenda".*** This revelation will become clearer as we journey through the pages of this book.

PREFACE

On the 16th of June 2019, the words "THE BLESSEDNNESS OF BARRENNESS" pierced through my spirit and soul, defying the ambience of the Sunday service. Instantly I knew a title has been delivered to me for the blessing of the barren. And immediately the Holy Spirit began to weave scriptures in my spirit, laying the foundation for this highly inspired book. Before the moment I heard the words, I have never heard that barrenness is a blessing but guess what? I didn't feel any doubt when I heard these words; all I felt was joy in my spirit. Instinctively, I knew a title has just been delivered to me for the blessing of the barren. I knew that God wants to reveal His truth about barrenness to His precious people.

This divine message titled *"The Blessedness of Barrenness"* is what I have put together in a book for the blessing of those who have been called barren. That he that reads it may run and fulfil purpose.

From scriptures, we are made to understand that *"The secret things belong unto the LORD our God: but those things which are revealed belong unto us and to our children for ever, **that we may do all the words of the law"** (Deuteronomy 29:29). In other words, the deep secrets of God are revealed to us to help us do God's will. The purpose of barrenness has been kept a secret right from creation but God has chosen to reveal it to us at this time, how that barrenness is a blessing in disguise. Perhaps in fulfilment of the prophecy of our Lord Jesus Christ, that the day will come when people shall say, *"**Blessed are the barren,** and the wombs that never bare, and the paps which never gave suck"*. I can tell you verily, that the time has come for people to start calling the barren blessed. Now is the time to say to the barren, *"Blessed art thou among women and blessed is the fruit of thy womb"*.

Therefore,

*Sing, O barren, thou that didst not bear; break forth into singing, and cry aloud, thou that didst not travail with child: for more are the children of the desolate than the children of the married wife, saith the LORD. With faith, enlarge the place of thy tent, and stretch forth the curtains of thine habitations: spare not, lengthen thy cords, and strengthen thy stakes; For thou shalt break forth on the right hand and on the left; and **thy seed shall inherit the Gentiles, and make the desolate cities to be inhabited**. Fear not; for thou shalt not be ashamed: neither be thou confounded; for thou shalt not be put to shame: for thou shalt forget the shame of thy youth, and shalt not remember the reproach of thy widowhood any more. For the mountains shall depart, and the hills be removed; but my kindness shall not depart from thee, neither shall the covenant of my peace be removed, saith the LORD that hath mercy on thee. And **all thy children shall be taught of the LORD; and great shall be the peace of thy children.***

Dear precious daughter of Zion, rejoice for the time has come for you to bring forth your blessed and precious seed.

Rejoice O barren, for through the pages of this book you will discover how **special** you are to God.

It's important to note that **the blessedness of barrenness is not an ordinary book; it is a divine message to the barren** in this last days.

INTRODUCTION

Barrenness, the inability of a woman to bear children, is perceived by many as a curse but I am glad to let you know that there is one kind of barrenness that is not a curse but a blessing in disguise.

You may begin to wonder, what is blessed about barrenness? Or how can barrenness be a blessing to anyone? Well, that is why you have this highly inspired book in your hands. As you read through the pages of this book, your eyes of understanding will be opened to how barrenness is a blessing.

From the Holy Scriptures we see that barrenness is completely against God's will for mankind. In the beginning when God created man, His first word to man was a word of blessing, God said to man **"Be fruitful and multiply"**. God's will for mankind is to be fruitful in child bearing. Barrenness is not God's will or desire for mankind and it will never be. However, we see that though barrenness is not God's will for man yet it could be a part of God's plan for mankind. It's important to note that there is a difference between God's plan and God's will. For instance, it is not God's will that His children should be poor or suffer any pain. But note that in God's plan for the salvation of mankind, God had to allow the Lord Jesus to be poor and to suffer pain that we through His suffering may be saved from sin, sickness and poverty (1Peter 2:24, 2 Corinthians

8:9). I believe the barrenness of Sarah and other matriarchs in scriptures is in God's plan for them and for all mankind. The Lord Jesus tells us how that some people are born eunuchs (in other words created as eunuchs by God from the womb), for the sake of the Kingdom of God.

*Matthew 19:12. For **there are some eunuchs, which were so born from their mother's womb**: and there are some eunuchs, which were made eunuchs of men: and there be eunuchs, which have made themselves eunuchs **for the kingdom of heaven's sake**. He that is able to receive it, let him receive it.*

A eunuch is a man who cannot bear children. The word eunuch applies to both men and women. Just as the word man in scriptures often refers to both gender. If God would create a man as a eunuch for the sake of the kingdom of God, then it is a part of God's plan because God has a plan and purpose for everything He creates.

Looking at God's creation we see that God has a purpose for creating even the minutest organism on the earth. For instance, without the microorganism bacteria there would be no decomposition. Bacteria may be insignificantly tiny or invisible to the naked eyes yet it is in God's plan as a means to get rid of waste products from the surface of the earth. Note that, the process of decomposition by bacteria may be messy, nasty and unpleasant, yet in that unpleasantness its purpose is being fulfilled. In the same vain barrenness may not be pleasant, nevertheless it is fulfilling its purpose. Like the insignificantly tiny bacteria we may not see how barrenness is fulfilling a purpose, nonetheless it does.

The bacteria and other microorganisms are God's medium for cleaning the earth of biological junks. The cleaning process may look unpleasant, dirty and even contrary to purpose at the beginning but with time it's purpose, worth and enrichment becomes more visible. And at the appointed time the bacteria cleans the earth of its junks and brings the earth to an enriched or glorified state.

A barren womb is like the earth undergoing a biological cleansing process, it's enrichment, worth, visibility and fulfilment is tied to time. Barrenness may look contrary to purpose but at the appointed time it's purpose and worth is made visible. And like the product of an enriched earth, the product of a barren womb is always a gracious and glorified seed.

It's important to note that serving God and the interest of His kingdom delivers from barrenness (Exodus 23:25-26). When you are serving God faithfully and you still remain barren, there is more to that barrenness. It simply means that God has called you to what I refer to as **"The Ministry of Barrenness"**. God does not delay in answering the prayers of his faithful children, if God delays in answering their prayers, it is for a reason. God himself has said ***that before they call, I will answer; and while they are yet speaking, I will hear.***

For any faithful servant of God to be asking God for the fruit of the womb for as long as ten years without God granting their request is an indication that they have been called to the ministry of barrenness.

Hear what the Holy Scripture says...

Proverbs 3:27. Withhold not good from them to whom it is due, when it is in the power of thine hand to do it.
28. Say not unto thy neighbour, Go, and come again, and to morrow I will give; when thou hast it by thee.

God has the power to give children to the barren; He will not withhold it from them to whom it is due. He will not say I will give you children in the next five years when He has the power to give them to you now, unless there is a purpose for the delay.

Beloved in Christ, this book is written to enlighten the eyes of the barren to see the ultimate purpose of barrenness, that barrenness is a blessing and not a curse. By the time you finish reading this book, you will discover that barrenness is not what to be ashamed of but what to be proud of. You will see that barrenness is indeed a blessing in disguise.

Chapter 1

CAUSES/TYPES OF BARRENNESS

In the realm of the spirit three personalities have control over man. They include God, the Devil and Man himself. When it concerns barrenness, these three personalities play a key role in causing barrenness in the life of man.

In this chapter, we would consider five different causes of barrenness.

1. **God ordained barrenness or the barrenness of purpose.**

This kind of barrenness is a calling. I call it the **calling of barrenness**. *The calling of barrenness is a call to fulfil the purpose of bearing a special child with a divine mandate of leadership.* It is important to note that people with this kind of barrenness have a calling or purpose to bear a special breed of children that will be influential in their time. This kind of barrenness is common with those who faithfully serve God.

Women with the calling of barrenness have a special womb (different from that of other women) which I refer to as *the called womb, the covenant womb or the kingly womb.*

I refer to the seeds (sperm) from the men with this calling as the kingly seeds. I refer to the children of those with the calling of barrenness as the kingly priests, kingly seeds or called seeds.

Those with this kind of barrenness have their wombs closed by God for a reason; some were created barren by God or born barren to fulfil a purpose.

*1 Samuel 1:5. But unto Hannah he gave a worthy portion; for he loved Hannah: but **the LORD had shut up her womb.***

Note importantly, that the devil has no hand in this kind of barrenness. In truth, the devil cannot touch the womb of these ones because their womb has already been touched and anointed by God to fulfil a purpose.

Our focus in this book is on the God ordained barrenness otherwise referred to as *"the barrenness of purpose or the calling of barrenness"*. This is the only type of barrenness that is a blessing, so when I talk about the blessedness of barrenness, I am referring to the barrenness of purpose. It is important to make this distinction so that the purpose and content of this book is not misunderstood.

In this kind of barrenness the husbands are always healthy and fruitful, it is the women that are often affected because God shuts their womb. We see this truth in the life of the first couple with the call of barrenness, Abraham and Sarah. Note that Sarah was barren but Abraham was fruitful and that was why he was able to have Ishmael through Hagar. In our contemporary time, when the couple with this call go for medical examination, the man will be found to be fertile whereas the woman's fertility may be difficult to diagnose or she may be diagnosed as infertile. Interestingly, the fruitfulness of the man and the unfruitfulness of the woman can serve as a sign or indicator that the couple have been chosen by God to fulfil the calling of barrenness.

It is important to note that the women with this kind of barrenness are not destined to die barren, they always bring forth at the appointed time. Therefore, if you fall into this category, find comfort in these words, that **"You are not destined to die barren, but to bring forth your own special breed of children at the appointed time. God has called you to fulfil His special purpose, therefore by this revelation you shall not die barren"**.

God always remembers those with the calling of barrenness for good. He remembered Sarah, Rachel, Hannah etc. **The God who remembered Hannah and Rachel, He will remember you also at the appointed time**.

1 Samuel 1:5. But unto Hannah he gave a worthy portion; for he loved Hannah: but **the LORD had shut up her womb.**
19. And they rose up in the morning early, and worshipped before the LORD, and returned, and came to their house to Ramah: and Elkanah knew Hannah his wife; and the **LORD remembered her.**

Genesis 30:22. And **God remembered Rachel,** *and God hearkened to her,* **and opened her womb.**
23. And she conceived, and bare a son; and said, God hath

taken away my reproach:

God always remembers those with the calling of barrenness, nevertheless we must always remind Him in prayers.

Its important to note that the cause of a barrenness is what determines if the barrenness becomes a blessing to the beneficiary or not. Only the God ordained barrenness or the barrenness of purpose results in a blessing.

2. Punishment for taking a covenant womb.

God can bring barrenness upon a family as a punishment for taking a covenant womb from her covenant husband. A covenant womb is a womb that has been covenanted or ordained by God to carry the seed of a particular person. A covenant womb can also be referred to as a Called womb. Women who have the calling of barrenness are the only women who have the called or covenant womb. Sarah was the first woman with the calling of barrenness. Her womb was covenanted to Abraham to carry the promised seed Isaac, which was the reason she was barren in the first place because of the special nature of her womb. The conception of Isaac was not all about Abraham's seed but also about Sarah's womb, otherwise Ishmael could have been the promised seed of Abraham. But because Ishmael was not borne by Sarah's womb (the covenant womb for the promised seed Isaac) he was not accepted as the covenant seed.

It's important to note that **when God wants to send His special breed of servants to the earth, He separates and**

calls a man and a woman for this purpose. Abraham and Sarah were called and separated by God to bring forth Isaac to the earth for the blessing of mankind, ***for in Abraham's seed shall all the nations of the earth be blessed*** (*Genesis 22:18*).

That established, now you will understand why God threatened to kill Abimelech when he tried to marry Sarah. Sarah's womb was destined to carry Abraham's covenant seed not Abimelech's seed. Abimelech by trying to take Sarah to be his wife was trying to change God's plan for Abraham and Sarah. And his household got punished for it with barrenness until Abraham prayed for them.

Genesis 20:17. So Abraham prayed unto God: and God healed Abimelech, and his wife, and his maidservants; and they bare children.
18. ***For the LORD had fast closed up all the wombs of the house of Abimelech, because of Sarah Abraham's wife.***

Abimelech unknowingly took Abraham's wife thinking she was his sister, yet that did not stop God from punishing him. That a man ignorantly takes a covenant womb is not an excuse for him not to be punished by God.

However, God often warns those in this class of barrenness, letting them know where they have erred, so they can make amends and be restored.
Interestingly, those with this kind of barrenness can easily be healed when they take heed to God's warning.

3. Self inflicted barrenness/impotence

This kind of barrenness is caused by man himself. Man can bring barrenness upon himself and family by indulging in sexual immorality. When a man has sex with his uncle's wife, he brings barrenness upon himself and the woman. He becomes impotent and the woman (i.e. his uncle's wife) becomes barren for life. Also when a man has sex with his brothers wife, he also brings barrenness upon himself and his brothers wife, he becomes impotent and his brothers wife become barren.

*Leviticus 20:20. And **if a man shall lie with his uncle's wife**, he hath uncovered his uncle's nakedness: they shall bear their sin; they shall die childless.*
*21. And **if a man shall take his brother's wife**, it is an unclean thing: he hath uncovered his brother's nakedness; they shall be childless.*

In truth, barrenness can come as a result of sexual immorality and promiscuity, no wonder the bible admonishes us to flee sexual lust.

It's important to note that those with this kind of barrenness die barren. And in this kind of barrenness both the man and the woman are infertile/barren. This kind of barrenness has no remedy, except of course God decides to have mercy on those concerned.

As a word of caution, it's worthy of note that, the consequence of any act of sexual immorality often outweighs the short time of pleasure, therefore beware of sexual immorality.

4. Devil inflicted barrenness.

Some kind of barrenness are caused by demonic afflictions. This kind of barrenness is what I refer to as devil inflicted barrenness or barrenness caused by demonic affliction. This kind of barrenness is caused by the devil and his agents. The devil can cause barrenness, in truth he specialises in stealing what God has given to man. The Lord Jesus made us to understand that the devil as a thief comes to steal what God has given to man.

John 10:10. The thief cometh not, but for to steal, and to kill, and to destroy: I am come that they might have life, and that they might have it more abundantly.

One of the things the devil comes to steal, kill and destroy is the fruitfulness of man. The devil comes to steal, kill and destroy the fruitfulness of mankind and make them barren. One of the ways the devil steals, kills and destroys man's fruitfulness is through miscarriages.

Those with this kind of barrenness often have miscarriages, they conceive but then have miscarriage. This miscarriage is the outcome of the Devil's activity. Not all miscarriages are due to a medical condition; most miscarriages are a product of the Devils activity of stealing, killing and destroying babies in the womb.

Also those with this kind of barrenness often have stillbirths, while some don't even conceive at all. In this kind of barrenness, both the man and the woman can be affected. The reason for unfruitfulness could be from either the man or the woman, unlike in the barrenness of purpose where only the woman is unfruitful.

This kind of barrenness often evades medical diagnosis and defy medical treatment. Since the cause of the barrenness is spiritual, it would only take a spiritual approach to resolve the condition. Jesus is the only answer to such barrenness, he is the only spiritual surgeon that has the treatment for such barrenness.

This kind of barrenness is common with those who have not made Jesus the Lord and Saviour of their life and who have not been saved from their sins. This is because as long as a man remains sinful, he remains under the dominion of the devil and can be afflicted with barrenness by the devil at any time.

1 John 3:8. **He that committeth sin is of the devil***; for the devil sinneth from the beginning.* **For this purpose the Son of God was manifested, that he might destroy the works of the devil.**

Interestingly, this kind of barrenness can be remedied and only Jesus can remedy the situation. Only Jesus can deliver man from the barrenness caused by the devil, for "**For this purpose the Son of God was manifested, that he might destroy the works of the devil.**

It's important to note that those afflicted with this kind of barrenness can die barren if they don't surrender to Jesus and get saved.

From the holy scriptures we are made to understand that, until we submit or surrender to God, our prayers of resistance against the devil and his activities will end in futility and will not avail much.

*James 4:7. **Submit yourselves therefore to God. Resist the devil, and he will flee from you.***
*8. **Draw nigh to God, and he will draw nigh to you.** Cleanse your hands, ye sinners; and purify your hearts, ye double minded.*
9. Be afflicted, and mourn, and weep: let your laughter be turned to mourning, and your joy to heaviness.
10. Humble yourselves in the sight of the Lord, and he shall lift you up.

For the devil to flee when we resist him, we must be under the care and Lordship of Jesus Christ. We must purge ourselves of every form of sin, submit ourselves to God and trust Him to help us.

For those who have gone to demonic shrines and evil temples to seek the fruit of the womb, you must repent of your sins, be remorseful, mourn, weep, afflict yourself in fasting, submit to Jesus and surrender yourself to His Lordship. As you draw near to God He will also draw near to you and as you cleanse yourself He will further cleanse you, lift you up and grant you your desires.

After you have surrendered to the Lordship of Jesus the next thing to do is to faithfully serve God because it is in serving God that the womb is insured, secured and blessed.

*Exodus 23:25. And ye shall **serve the LORD your God**, and he shall bless thy bread, and thy water; and I will take sickness away from the midst of thee.*
*26. There shall **nothing cast their young, nor be barren**, in thy land: the number of thy days I will fulfil.*

Serving God insures and secures the womb thus preventing the devil from stealing, killing and destroying our fruitfulness.

Those with this kind of barrenness will need to exercise great faith in God in other to come out of barrenness into fruitfulness.

5. Medically induced barrenness.

Some women become barren due to long term medical procedures like abortions. Some become barren due to some medical conditions like hormonal imbalance, pelvic inflammatory disease (PID), fibroids, low sperm count, heavy use of alcohol, old age etc. to mention a few. Medical conditions could lead to unfruitfulness but not all unfruitfulness are caused by medical conditions.
This kind of barrenness can affect both the man and the woman. The reason for barrenness among a couple could either be from the man or from the woman.
Importantly, this kind of barrenness can be diagnosed and treated medically. This kind of barrenness may not require any spiritual approach to resolve it, however engaging a spiritual approach could facilitate the entire healing process.

In closing this chapter, it's important to know this truth that, when you are barren as a woman or a man, you will be mocked, provoked and made to weep, but instead of fighting or quarreling with those that mock you, let all that anger and bitterness be channeled to God in prayer like Hannah exemplified.

1 Samuel 1:5. But unto Hannah he gave a worthy portion; for he loved Hannah: but the LORD had shut up her womb.
*6. And **her adversary also provoked her sore**, for to make her fret, because the LORD had shut up her womb.*
7. And as he did so year by year, when she went up to the house of the LORD, so she provoked her; therefore she wept, and did not eat.
*10. And **she was in bitterness of soul, and prayed unto the LORD, and wept sore**.*

Chapter 2

BARRENNESS AS A DIVINE CALLING

"Sing, O barren, for the LORD hath called thee…"
~ Isaiah 54:1-2

Barrenness is a CALL to fulfil purpose. It is a high calling of God. A CALL is a moral duty, work or assignment that you are obliged to perform for spiritual, moral or legal reasons. In other words a CALL is a specific purpose or assignment that God has designed or created us to fulfil. A calling can therefore be referred to as the particular assignment, vocation or purpose for which someone is created. Interestingly, just as the purpose of a product cannot be determined by the product but by the producer, in the same vain we as God's products cannot determine our purpose, God our Creator determines our purpose.

Barrenness is the identity of those who have the call of barrenness. We may not know the purpose we are created to fulfil, but there are things that could serve as markers or pointers to our God ordained purpose or calling in life. Interestingly, barrenness is the marker (pointer) to the purpose of those who are created to fulfil the call of barrenness.

From the Holy Scriptures we have seen that God created some people to be barren in other to fulfil His purpose. (Matthew 19:12).

There are special breed of women who are created to give birth to a special breed of men, and these special breed of women unfortunately are designed to be barren before they bring forth the special breed of men. The identity of this special breed of women is barrenness, just as the identity of the special breed of eunuchs is impotence. Barrenness is not a curse but rather an identity of a great calling, purpose or destiny. When we see barrenness as a calling, we would see and understand how that *"all things work together for the good of those who are called to fulfil God's purpose"*.

The scriptures below will help our understanding.

*Romans 8:28. And we know that all things work together for good to them that love God, to them who are the **called according to his purpose.***
*30. Moreover whom he did **predestinate**, them he also **called**: and whom he called, them he also justified: and whom he justified, them he also glorified.*

*2 Timothy 1:9. Who hath saved us, and **called us with an holy calling**, not according to our works, but **according to his own purpose** and grace, **which was given** us in Christ Jesus **before the world began,***

God will always glorify the called.

Predestination refers to an established purpose assigned to someone before they were born. It is the purpose for which one is created. Everyone is called according to the purpose he was created. If you were not created barren you cannot fulfil the purpose of bringing forth to the earth the special breed of men that God has destined to send to the earth. The story of Jeremiah shows us a clear picture of predestination at work.

Jeremiah 1:5. Before I formed thee in the belly I knew thee; and before thou camest forth out of the womb I sanctified thee, and I ordained thee a prophet unto the nations.

The call of barrenness is not a choice, it is a heavenly factory fitted call, designed from the source. God the Creator purposefully created the womb of these women to be barren even before they were born. The women with this call are born barren, they did not make themselves barren, so God takes responsibility for their barrenness and makes it up to them with the blessing of a great seed at the appointed time, as seen in Isaiah 54.

Prophet Isaiah by divine inspiration reveals to us how that barrenness is a call.

*Isaiah 54:1. **Sing, O barren**, thou that didst not bear; break forth into singing, and cry aloud, thou that didst not travail with child: for more are the children of the desolate than the children of the married wife, saith the LORD.*
*6. **For the LORD hath called thee** as a woman forsaken and grieved in spirit, and a wife of youth, when thou wast refused, saith thy God.*

Sing, O barren, for the LORD hath called thee...

The call of barrenness is a call to be forsaken and to grieve for an appointed time after which it will be overturned. Barren women often grief and are forsaken because the duo (shame and reproach) are components of the call of barrenness. The call of barrenness is a special call that requires patience and forbearance. However the joy and glory of fulfilling the call supersedes the sorrow that may be encountered in the process as documented in Isaiah 54.

*Isaiah 54:3. For thou shalt break forth on the right hand and on the left; and **thy seed shall inherit the Gentiles, and make the desolate cities to be inhabited.***
*4. Fear not; for **thou shalt not be ashamed: neither be thou confounded**; for thou shalt not be put to shame: for **thou shalt forget the shame of thy youth**, and **shalt not remember the reproach of thy widowhood** any more.*
*5. For **thy Maker is thine husband**; the LORD of hosts is his name; and thy Redeemer the Holy One of Israel; The God of the whole earth shall he be called.*
*11. O thou afflicted, tossed with tempest, and not comforted, behold, **I will lay thy stones with fair colours, and lay thy foundations with sapphires.***
*12. And **I will make thy windows of agates, and thy gates of carbuncles, and all thy borders of pleasant stones.***
*13. And **all thy children shall be taught of the LORD;** and great shall be the peace of thy children.*
*14. **In righteousness shalt thou be established: thou shalt be far from oppression;** for thou shalt not fear: and from terror; for it shall not come near thee.*

Permit me to outline the benefits of the call of barrenness from the above scriptures.

BENEFITS OF THE CALL OF BARRENNESS

These can also be seen as **compensations** for being saddled with the call of barrenness.

i. *Your children shall be great leaders and influencers in their time. Men that will provide shelter and sustenance to cities and nations. Men that are nation builders.*

ii. *You will not be put to shame or experience shame after that you have fulfilled the call.*

iii. *The joy and glory of the call will make you forget whatever shame and reproach you may have suffered in the past.*

iv. *God becomes your husband. Imagine God as your husband, it simply means you will never lack any good thing. Oh! I can only imagine how perfect your life will be having a perfect husband like God. Many women wish they could have a perfect husband but interestingly only those with the call of barrenness can have the perfect husband, God.*

v. *God will lay your stones with fair colours, and lay your foundations with sapphires. In other words, God will make you all round beautiful and pleasant.*

vi. *Your children will be taught by God. Imagine your children being taught by God, no wonder such children have the mantle of divine leadership. When your children are taught by God they will not only be super-*

wise but they will operate with the wisdom of God in all things.

vii.   *Your children will enjoy great peace.*

viii. *God will establish you in righteousness. Which in turn guarantees heaven for you.*

ix.   *You will not be oppressed or terrorised by the powers of darkness because God, your perfect husband watches over you.*

x.   *And many more.*

Imagine the kind of blessings that accompany this call. I would like you to take some time to think about these blessings that follow this great and high calling. All these benefits however come at a cost.

OUR ADVERSE EXPERIENCES IS OFTEN A REFLECTION OF OUR CALLING

*Isaiah 51:2. Look unto Abraham your father, and unto Sarah that bare you: for **I called him alone**, and blessed him, and increased him.*

3. For the LORD shall comfort Zion: he will comfort all her waste places; and he will make her wilderness like Eden, and her desert like the garden of the LORD; joy and gladness shall be found therein, thanksgiving, and the voice of melody.

God called Abraham to fruitfulness, He called him to be a father of nations. But interestingly that call was to be fulfilled through the call of barrenness. For Abraham to be made fruitful he had to first experience barrenness. We see that the call of fruitfulness was preceded by the call of barrenness. I realise from scriptures that often we are made to experience what we are called to fulfil. That is, we are made to experience the problem for which we are created to proffer solution. Moses was called and ordained from the womb to deliver and bring salvation to the children of Israel and that was to happen through signs and wonders but note that he had to first experience the miracles he was called to perform.

Exodus 4:5. That they may believe that the LORD God of their fathers, the God of Abraham, the God of Isaac, and the God of Jacob, hath appeared unto thee.
*6. And the LORD said furthermore unto him, **Put now thine hand into thy bosom. And he put his hand into his bosom: and when he took it out, behold, his hand was leprous as snow.***
*7. And he said, **Put thine hand into thy bosom again. And he put his hand into his bosom again; and plucked it out of his bosom, and, behold, it was turned again as his other flesh.***
8. And it shall come to pass, if they will not believe thee, neither hearken to the voice of the first sign, that they will believe the voice of the latter sign.

Whatever difficulty or challenging situation we experience in life is a reflection of our calling. The barrenness of Sarah was a reflection of her calling. Abraham was called to be a father of nations but there was no way he could become a father of nations without his wife Sarah who was also called to be a mother of nations by reason of her union with Abraham.

Genesis 17:1. And when Abram was ninety years old and nine, the LORD appeared to Abram, and said unto him, I am the Almighty God; walk before me, and be thou perfect.

*2. And I will make my covenant between me and thee, **and will multiply thee exceedingly.***

*4. As for me, behold, my covenant is with thee, **and thou shalt be a father of many nations.***

15. And God said unto Abraham, As for Sarai thy wife, thou shalt not call her name Sarai, but Sarah shall her name be.

*16. And I will bless her, and give thee a son also of her: yea, I will bless her, and **she shall be a mother of nations; kings of people shall be of her.***

18. And Abraham said unto God, O that Ishmael might live before thee!

*19. And God said, **Sarah thy wife shall bear thee a son indeed**; and thou shalt call his name Isaac: **and I will establish my covenant with him for an everlasting covenant, and with his seed after him.***

20. And as for Ishmael, I have heard thee: Behold, I have blessed him, and will make him fruitful, and will multiply him exceedingly; twelve princes shall he beget, and I will make him a great nation.

*21. **But my covenant will I establish with Isaac, which Sarah shall bear unto thee** at this set time in the next year.*

In God's design every call requires the negative reflection of the call to prepare the called for the call. Note that the negative reflection of fruitfulness is barrenness, the negative reflection of prosperity is poverty, the negative reflection of holiness is sin etc., these negative reflections are evident in the lives of many great and anointed people in our time who have made it to their promised land. My father in the LORD

Bishop David Oyedepo for instance who today is named among the top wealthiest servants of God in the world, once suffered lack in the early years of his life and ministry. Joyce Meyer whom God is using today to reach out to the abused and depressed once suffered abuse and depression in her life. The list of examples are too numerous to mention.

In photography it is seen that every colourful picture begins with reversed colours or a negative image, the reversed or negative image serves as a foundation for the colourful picture. So also every colourful destiny or call begins with a reversed negative image.

Have you ever wondered why the road to the Promised Land passed through the wilderness? Similarly, the road to the fruitful land passes through the barren land, hence those with the call of barrenness experience barrenness on their way to fruitfulness. It's important to note that the wilderness is not the destination but a side attraction on the way to the Promised Land; rather the Promised Land is the destination. In the same manner, barrenness is not the destination but a side attraction on the way to fruitfulness. Fruitfulness is the ultimate destination for those with the call of barrenness.

God had a good and fruitful land for the children of Israel, a land that flows with milk, honey and all the goodies of the earth, yet to get to the promised land God had to take the children of Israel through the wilderness, a barren land where they had to eat only one kind of meal and be pruned by hunger. The wilderness/barrenness experience work together for the good of the called.

THE HALLMARK OF EVERY DIVINE CALLING

To understand the depth of our calling and to make the most of it, I have added this section about the hallmark of every divine calling. An understanding of this will help the called to know and understand the worth and value of their calling and also to pursue their calling to the point of fulfilment.

1. EVERY DIVINE CALLING IS A HEAVENLY CALLING.

*Hebrews 3:1. Wherefore, holy brethren, **partakers of the heavenly calling**, consider the Apostle and High Priest of our profession, Christ Jesus;*

Every divine calling is a heavenly calling. Every divine calling is given from heaven and it points men to heaven. Every heavenly calling points men to God and to heaven. Any calling that does not point men to heaven or to God is not a heavenly calling.

The Lord Jesus Christ is the High Priest of every calling. He is the overall head of all who have the heavenly calling. When we understand that our calling (no matter how little it looks) is a heavenly calling meant to point men to heaven and to God, we would understand that through our calling God has put a premium or value on us and we would make the most of it.

2. EVERY CALLING OF GOD IS CUSTOM-MADE FROM HEAVEN'S FACTORY

God equips the called right from the womb. Our calling is put in us as we are being created by God in the womb. Just as God puts in us some abilities, gifts, talents etc so also does God put in us our various calling. We are therefore born with our calling, it is there from when we are born until we die. No wonder the gifts and calling of God are without repentance.

Romans 11:29. For the gifts and calling of God are without repentance.

When God has called a man to fulfil a purpose, He doesn't change or take away the calling from the man. That seed of purpose remains in the man from birth to death. But like every seed, the calling of a man is only visible to all when it is nurtured. Until the seed of purpose is watered and nurtured men will not see or recognise the calling. If the seed is not nurtured, it won't bring forth fruits for men to see the calling. We water and nurture the seed of purpose by following God's plan for our lives through the counsel or leading of His word. Purposes are established by counsels, therefore for any purpose to be seen, known or established we need to seek the counsel and leading of the Holy Spirit the revealer of all truth and purposes.

Proverbs 15:22. Without counsel purposes are disappointed: but in the multitude of counsellers they are established.

Proverbs 20:18. **Every purpose is established by counsel: and with good advice make war.**

God has a timeline for every purpose and by seeking the counsel and leading of God we are able to discover God's timeline for our purpose and fulfil it at the appointed time, for to every thing there is a season, and a time to every purpose under the heaven (Ecclesiastes 3:1).

There is a seed of purpose that God has put in every man and that seed of purpose is never taken away from man. However that seed can be unnurtured, malnourished and unfruiful, thus making it invisible to all. The fact that a calling is not visible doesn't mean that it is not there. Whenever the seed is nurtured, it brings forth fruits and become visible for all to see. The calling of many is not visible because they are not nurturing it by seeking and following God's instructions and counsel.

However for those who are nurturing their calling, we must understand that God has a timeline for every calling to be fulfilled. For instance, every new born child has in him/her the ability to produce sperm cells/eggs but until that child is about fifteen years of age before they can start manifesting that sperm and egg production. No matter how the child tries at five years, they will never be able to fulfil that calling, though they have in them the ability. No wonder the Lord Jesus said to His mother when it was not yet time for the fulfilment or manifestation of His calling, *"Mine hour is not yet come" (John 2:4).*

The timeline of fulfilment of purpose is always different for the called and for those without the call. For those with the calling of barrenness the time for the fulfilment of their calling for them to become fruitful takes longer time than that of others without the calling and that is why those without the calling can put to birth every year if they want. The Lord Jesus speaking to His brothers in John seven verse six said, **"My time is not yet come: but your time is always ready".**

I see that, for those with the calling of barrenness the appointed time for their fruitfulness is average of twenty years after marriage. Therefore if you are still in the tenth year keep waiting on God, stay planted in His house, or perhaps you are in the twentieth year, then start enlarging your tent, for your appointed time is here.

3. GOD DOES NOT CALL THE QUALIFIED, HE QUALIFIES THE CALLED.

No one deserves to be called. We are not called because we deserve or merit it. Understand that the fact that you are called is a reflection that you are foolish and weak. Nonetheless, God called you to make you wise, strong and noble. Understand that your calling is what makes you wise and strong, that without it you will return to your foolish and weak state. If we understand this we would not let our calling make us proud and arrogant.

God does not call the qualified rather He calls the unqualified and qualifies those He calls. No wonder it is written in Romans 8:30 that, *they whom He called, them He also justified: and whom He justified, them He also glorifies.* If God calls the qualified He would not need to justify them. Let's see what God through apostle Paul said about our calling.

*1 Corinthians 1:26. For **ye see your calling**, brethren, how that not many wise men after the flesh, not many mighty, **not many noble, are called:***
27. But God hath chosen the foolish things of the world to confound the wise; and God hath chosen the weak things of the world to confound the things which are mighty;
28. And base things of the world, and things which are despised, hath God chosen, yea, and things which are not, to bring to nought things that are:
29. That no flesh should glory in his presence.

Never let the greatness of your calling get into your head. We must always acknowledge the truth that we are the most unqualified for the job, that we are nothing without the grace and calling of God, in truth we are the foolish, weak and base things that without the calling of God we would be despised. We must see that our calling is what gives us value on the earth. When we see that our calling is what gives us value and worth among men, we would give more attention to it. The calling of God upon a man is what can turn an ordinary illiterate fisherman like Peter to a highly respected world religious leader. The calling of God is what can turn a murderous and sinful man like Saul to a highly spiritual, holy and miracle working apostle Paul. The calling of God adds value to our life. Your calling is meant to add value to your life. May your calling add and give value to your life. Amen.

As a called, if you want to be valued on the earth, you must pursue your calling passionately. Until we start fulfilling our calling we would not have value on the earth, rather we would be despised. Fulfilling our calling brings us out of despicability and despondency.

Many called may look weak, lowly or even foolish yet God chooses them that He may show His power and glory through them. Concerning Paul the apostle, it was said that his bodily presence was weak and his speech contemptible yet his words were weighty and powerful (2 Corinthians 10:10). Apostle Peter was a timid, poor and illiterate man but his calling empowered him to speak boldly and powerfully.

The outward appearance of the called is often of little or no value to God. What matters to God is what He puts inside the vessel we refer to as the body or flesh. Many people despise the called and his message because of their outward appearance. My candid advice, "Never despise the message of the called". The wise men of the earth that despised the message of Noah discovered their foolishness too late. Never despise the message contained in this book. This is not an ordinary book, but a divine message to those with the call of barrenness.

4. WE ARE CALLED TO SERVE GOD.

We are called to be servants of God and to do His bidding at every point in time. It doesn't matter the nature of the call, it will still point you towards service. The Lord Jesus, though God, yet He said, I am among you as He that serves. Now hear what apostle Paul has to say.

*1 Corinthians 7:20. **Let every man abide in the same calling wherein he was called.***
21. Art thou called being a servant? care not for it: but if thou mayest be made free, use it rather.
*22. For he that is called in the Lord, being a servant, is the Lord's freeman: likewise also **he that is called, being free, is Christ's servant.***
23. Ye are bought with a price; be not ye the servants of men.
*24. Brethren, **let every man, wherein he is called, therein abide with God.***

In whatever area we are called to serve, we must ensure we abide therein with God.

It is important to note that in any area of our calling God is our direct boss. We are accountable to Him and not to man. We must therefore carry God along in everything we are doing in our calling. If we carry God along in everything we do in our calling, we would avoid doing what God dislikes or go against His will and God in turn will direct our path.

5. WE MUST DILIGENTLY PURSUE OUR CALLING BY SEEKING THE NECESSARY GRACE OR VIRTUES REQUIRED FOR ITS FULFILMENT.

*2 Peter 1:5. And beside this, **giving all diligence, add to your faith virtue;** and to virtue knowledge;*
6. And to knowledge temperance; and to temperance patience; and to patience godliness;
7. And to godliness brotherly kindness; and to brotherly kindness charity.

8. *For if these things be in you, and abound, they make you that ye shall neither be barren nor unfruitful in the knowledge of our Lord Jesus Christ.*
9. *But he that lacketh these things is blind, and cannot see afar off, and hath forgotten that he was purged from his old sins.*
10. *Wherefore the rather, brethren, **give diligence to make your calling and election sure**: for if ye do these things, ye shall never fall:*
11. *For so an entrance shall be ministered unto you abundantly into the everlasting kingdom of our Lord and Saviour Jesus Christ.*

To fulfil any calling, faith, virtue, knowledge, temperance, patience, godliness, kindness and love is required. They are necessary ingredients required for the fulfilment of our calling. We must therefore diligently seek to have these **EIGHT** spiritual ingredients in us, as they will make it easy for us to fulfil our calling.

1. **FAITH**: Faith is the foundation of every calling, therefore have faith is God who created you and has called you to fulfil a purpose. It's important to also note that we must develop our faith in the area of our calling.

2. **VIRTUE**: Virtue is the quality of doing what is right and avoiding what is wrong. That is the quality of being good. Always do what is right and avoid whatever is wrong or sinful. Have moral excellence.
Virtue could also mean the inherent power of God. When the woman with the issue of blood touched the Lord Jesus, He said "virtue is gone out of me", in other words power or

anointing is gone out of me. We need the power to fulfil our calling; the Lord Jesus made us to understand that he was able to fulfil His calling because He had the power to lay down his life (John 10:18). We need the empowerment of the Holy Spirit to do both what is right (the will of God) and to fulfil our calling. We must diligently seek this empowerment.

3. **KNOWLEDGE**: Discover your calling by seeking the counsel of God through reading the Holy Scriptures. Seek knowledge about your calling. Read the bible to discover your calling, and read Holy Spirit inspired books about your calling to develop them.

4. **TEMPERANCE**: Temperance is the ability to avoid or abstain from excesses. It is to have self-control. Develop the ability to control yourself, your thoughts, your emotions, your actions, your words, your body etc.

5. **PATIENCE**: Patience is the ability to wait when purpose is delayed. We must learn to exercise patience when our calling is not yet visible or being fulfilled. Every calling has an appointed time; we need patience to wait for the appointed time of the fulfilment of our purpose and calling. *"For ye have need of patience, that, after ye have done the will of God, ye might receive the promise. For yet a little while, and he that shall come will come, and will not tarry"* (Hebrews 10:36-37). God is a God of patience; as such He does His things with patience and requires us to also be patient (Romans 15:5).

Those with the call of barrenness need patience the most. We remember how that Abraham (the man who had the first calling of barrenness) after he had patiently endured, he obtained the promise (Hebrews 6:13-15). The need for patience in the pursuit of our calling cannot be overemphasised for we are expected to run the race of our calling with patience (Hebrews 12:1).

6. **GODLINESS**: Godliness is a state of being holy or righteous. We are called unto godliness, *"for God has not called us unto uncleanness but unto holiness"*. Godliness profits, it is what makes our calling to be profitable and to yield the desired result, *"for godliness is profitable unto all things"*. Godliness is the fertiliser or catalyst that makes our calling to be productive. Those with the call of barrenness need this ingredient the most, for we know how that Abraham was righteous before God.

7. **KINDNESS**: Kindness is the quality of being warmhearted, considerate, sympathetic, generous and forgiving. Our calling is for the good of others, for in God's Kingdom we are called to serve. We must therefore be kind to generously give the best of our calling for the betterment of the life of others. When we pursue our calling for the good of others, our calling finds speedy and quick fulfilment. We see that Abraham's act of kindness hastened the fulfilment of the promise.

8. **LOVE**: Be love motivated, let the love of God and mankind direct your calling.

There are calling that have become barren and unfruitful, Yes! A calling can become barren or unfruitful when the necessary ingredients mentioned above are not in the life of the called. It takes the above fruits or ingredients for our calling not to be barren or unfruitful.

A man without the above ingredients will find it difficult to fulfil his God given calling. The ingredients above serve as nutrient for the nourishment of our calling. A man without these spiritual ingredients is like a plant sown on a ground without nutrients. Every calling must be nourished; any call without nourishment will not be fruitful. We need all the above ingredients to nourish our calling. Perhaps you have a great calling in your life, see that you nourish it with the above ingredients or nutrients.

The above ingredients or fruits empower us not to ever fall or fail in our God given calling. They secure our calling and make it steadfast and sure. We need this spiritual fruits if we must not fall or fail in our calling. Also importantly, having this spiritual fruits opens us up to greater dimensions of the manifestations of the Kingdom of God. It opens unto us greater grace and anointing for the fulfilment of our calling.

Keep adding the ingredients one after the other. Keep making diligent efforts to add one ingredient upon another. Love is the last of the ingredients we must acquire. When we acquire these virtues to a point that we are moved by love in the fulfilment of our calling, we come to a point of supernatural abundance of grace, power and anointing for the fulfilment of our calling. At this point fulfilling our calling becomes super-easy.

6. EVERY CALL OF THE MOST HIGH GOD IS A HIGH CALLING.

*Philippians 3:14. I press toward the mark for the prize of the **high calling of God** in Christ Jesus.*

A high calling is a calling that is greater than normal, it is a supernatural or supernormal calling. It is a calling that is given by God not by man. It is a calling that cannot be understood by the normal or natural senses neither can it be understood by science. This kind of calling can only be perceived, understood and fulfilled by following our spiritual senses and obeying spiritual laws. This calling operates beyond natural laws. It is designed, ordained, sponsored and powered by the supernatural. A high calling is of great or high importance to God no matter how little it may seem.

No call is better than another. In the eyes of God every call is important. In the eyes of God, the call of barrenness is as important as every other calling in the body of Christ.
Just as in the body the calling of the eye, though it's different from that of the hand, yet they both have their own unique importance in the body, so also is every calling in the body of Christ.

1 Corinthians 12:18. But now hath God set the members every one of them in the body, as it hath pleased him.
21. And the eye cannot say unto the hand, I have no need of thee: nor again the head to the feet, I have no need of you.
22. Nay, much more those members of the body, which seem to be more feeble, are necessary:
23. And those members of the body, which we think to be less honourable, upon these we bestow more abundant

honour; and our uncomely parts have more abundant comeliness.
27. Now ye are the body of Christ, and members in particular.
28. And God hath set some in the church, first apostles, secondarily prophets, thirdly teachers, after that miracles, then gifts of healings, helps, governments, diversities of tongues.

Each calling may be different but they all have the same high calling of God which is for the sustenance and glorification of the body of Christ.

7. WE MUST PRESS TOWARDS THE MARK OF OUR CALLING.

Every calling requires efforts, labour or hard work to find expression. It demands that the called take responsibility for the fulfilment of their calling.

Philippians 3:13. Brethren, I count not myself to have apprehended: but this one thing I do, forgetting those things which are behind, and reaching forth unto those things which are before,
*14. **I press toward the mark for the prize of the high calling of God in Christ Jesus.***

Never get satisfied with where you are or with what you have achieved in pursuit of your calling. It is said that good is the enemy of excellent. Apostle Paul said *"I count not myself to have apprehended: but this one thing I do, forgetting those things which are behind, and reaching forth unto those things which are before"*. In other words I have not fully achieved my goal, but I do this one thing, I forget what I have achieved so far and make efforts to achieve more.

It's important for us to know that even when the grace to pursue a vision, purpose or calling is released we still need to make efforts and take responsibility for the grace to bring forth. We need to labour or work hard to see our calling fulfilled.

Apostle Paul the man who understood the meaning of his calling and what it entails said...

*1 Corinthians 15:10. But by the grace of God I am what I am: and his grace which was bestowed upon me was not in vain; but **I laboured more abundantly** than they all: yet not I, but the grace of God which was with me.*

He said, I did not allow the grace of God upon my life to be in vain, I ensure that I labour and make efforts to see the grace of God bring forth in my life.

Grace is given to us for our advantage. However, for grace to be useful it has to be put to work. Grace without labour will not be of any advantage to us.

8. WE ARE CALLED TO PATIENTLY ENDURE GRIEF AND SUFFERING FOLLOWING THE FOOT STEPS OF JESUS

1 Peter 2:19. For this is thankworthy, if a man for conscience toward God endure grief, suffering wrongfully.
*21. For even **hereunto were ye called: because Christ also suffered for us, leaving us an example, that ye should follow his steps:***

We are not called to suffer, however, if the need arises for us to suffer grief for some time, we must endure it like Jesus did. People will mock you and despise you as a barren woman but you must endure it, knowing (especially now that you have this understanding) that the price or trophy of a kingly seed lies ahead.

9. OUR CALL SHOULD BE OUR PASSION

Apostle Paul was called to preach the gospel (Romans 1:1) and he put all of his passion into it.

*1 Corinthians 9:16. For though I preach the gospel, I have nothing to glory of: for necessity is laid upon me; yea, **woe is unto me, if I preach not the gospel**!*

Apostle Paul understood the value of his calling and he said, "Woe unto me if I preach not the gospel", he was highly passionate and dedicated to his call. For those with the call of barrenness, your watch word should be *"Woe unto me if I do not fulfil my calling"*. In otherwords, you must work hard towards fulfilling your calling, despising the shame and the pain. Instead of being ashamed of your calling because of your barrenness, rather let the barrenness be a thing of pride to you. Instead of feeling depressed, rather sing with joy, for the LORD hath said *"Sing, O barren"*. Be passionate about fulfilling your calling.

10. THE GOSPEL (THE WORD OF GOD) IS GOD'S TOOL FOR REVEALING OUR CALLING TO US.

God chose us before we were born, however He calls us through His word. We are chosen by default from God's factory and are called to know and pursue our purpose through the gospel.

2 Thessalonians 2:13. But we are bound to give thanks alway to God for you, brethren beloved of the Lord, because God hath from the beginning chosen you to salvation through sanctification of the Spirit and belief of the truth:
*14. **Whereunto he called you by our gospel**, to the obtaining of the glory of our Lord Jesus Christ.*

For you with the call of barrenness, I believe through the gospel in this book, you now know and understand your calling. May God continue to reveal the depth of this calling to you through His word of truth. Amen.

11. EVERY CALL OF GOD IS A HOLY CALLING

Every call is holy to God, it doesn't matter the call, be it a call to serve or a call to be served

*2 Timothy 1:9. Who hath saved us, and **called us with an holy calling**, not according to our works, but **according to his own purpose and grace**, which was given us in Christ Jesus before the world began,*

We are saved by Christ to fulfil the purpose for which we were created. Part of the reason the Lord Jesus came and died for us was to empower us with the grace we need to fulfil our calling.

12. WE ARE CALLED TO BE SAINTS, WE ARE CALLED TO BE HOLY.

Romans 1:6. Among whom are ye also the called of Jesus Christ:
*7. To all that be in Rome, beloved of God, **called to be saints**: Grace to you and peace from God our Father, and the Lord Jesus Christ.*

*1 Corinthians 1:2. Unto the church of God which is at Corinth, to them that are sanctified in Christ Jesus, **called to be saints**, with all that in every place call upon the name of Jesus Christ our Lord, both theirs and ours:*

*1 Peter 1:15. But **as he which hath called you is holy, so be ye holy** in all manner of conversation;*
16. Because it is written, Be ye holy; for I am holy.

*1 Thessalonians 4:7. For **God hath not called us unto uncleanness, but unto holiness.***

We are not called to be sinners but to be saints. What this simply means is that as the called we are not expected to be living in sin. We are called to live a sanctified life. We are expected to live holy just as He who has called us is holy. That you are chosen and called does not make you indispensable. If you refuse to comply with the Callers rules, you will be rejected. Remember, Esau how that he was chosen to have the call of the first born but trivialised his call and sold his birthright (calling) to satisfy his flesh. And when he eventually came to his senses and wanted his call back to fulfil it, it could not be restored even when he sought it carefully with tears, because he was rejected.

Now, let me say this at this point that, that thing which you are always hungry for (that sin which your flesh always desires), will one day ask you for your birthright (calling) and if you are not careful it will take your calling from you. Therefore be careful what you yield your flesh to. Note that Jacob (the deceiver), like the devil had been feeding Esau with the same red pottage for a long time. He waited until Esau got addicted to it before asking him to give his calling in exchange for the pottage.

*Genesis 25:30. And Esau said to Jacob, Feed me, I pray thee, with that **same** red pottage; for I am faint: therefore was his name called Edom.*
31. And Jacob said, Sell me this day thy birthright.

In the same manner, the devil keeps feeding the called with sin (fornication, adultery, bitterness etc) until one day he asks for their calling in exchange for the sin. Perhaps, Esau thought Jacob loved him all the while he was feeding him with the pottage not knowing that he was feeding him fat to take his most precious gift from him. That is how the devil keeps feeding the called with sin until he takes their precious calling from them. Those who are not disciplined and who cannot exercise control over their fleshly desires are at risk of selling off their calling. Note that the sin of Esau (or the pottage he ate) was synonymous with fornication and all kinds of profanity: uncleanness, perversions, masturbations, pornography, sexual immorality etc. (Hebrews 12:16-17)

13. WE MUST CAREFULLY AND STEADFASTLY FOLLOW THE PATH OF OUR CALLING

Every calling has a path, we must carefully follow that path. We must allow God lead us on the path of our calling. We must walk in our calling and not deviate from it. Apostle Paul gives us an example, that if you are called to the uncircumcised, stay with the uncircumcised, don't go to the circumcised and vice versa. If you are called to follow, don't try to lead, because the capacity to lead has not been put in you. Don't try to be wiser than God by adding to your calling or by pursuing another calling.

1 Corinthians 7:17. But as God hath distributed to every man, as the Lord hath called every one, so let him walk. And so ordain I in all churches.
*18. **Is any man called being circumcised? let him not become uncircumcised. Is any called in uncircumcision? let him not be circumcised.***
19. Circumcision is nothing, and uncircumcision is nothing, but the keeping of the commandments of God.
*20. **Let every man abide in the same calling wherein he was called.***
21. Art thou called being a servant? care not for it: but if thou mayest be made free, use it rather.
22. For he that is called in the Lord, being a servant, is the Lord's freeman: likewise also he that is called, being free, is Christ's servant.

24. Brethren, **let every man, wherein he is called, therein abide with God.**

Apostle Paul understood his calling and he pursued that single calling. And here's what he has to say.

Galatians 1:15. But when it pleased God, who separated me from my mother's womb, and called me by his grace,
16. To reveal his Son in me, that I might preach him among the heathen; immediately I conferred not with flesh and blood:

Apostle Paul followed his calling to the heathen or Gentiles and today Christ is revealed to the Gentiles by pursuing this single calling. The call of barrenness is a call that demands the same kind of commitment and pursuit. This call is not just in bringing forth the kingly seeds but also in nurturing them with the understanding of their purpose and calling.
Beloved in Christ, Let your eyes be single, so that your whole body can be full of light. When you are focused on your calling, you receive revelation, strength and divine enablement to fulfil the calling.

14. WE MUST SEE OUR CALLING AS A VOCATION

A vocation is a job, career, business, occupation or line of work. We must take our calling as a job. We must give it the kind of attention we would give to our job or business.

Ephesians 4:1. I therefore, the prisoner of the Lord, beseech you that ye walk worthy of **the vocation wherewith ye are called,**

Those with the call of barrenness must see their calling as a vocation. And give it the kind of attention we would give to our job, career or business. A business approach to your calling is what will make you achieve success in that calling. Even the Lord Jesus applied a business approach to the kingdom to achieve the kind of success He had.

15. ALL THINGS WORK TOGETHER FOR THE GOOD OF THE CALLED

*Romans 8:28. And we know that all things work together for good to them that love God, to them who are the **called according to his purpose.***

The unfruitfulness of the called barren is working together for their good. When you are called to fulfil God's purpose, be rest assured that God will not forsake you. Even when you are in a very difficult situation, be sure that God has a purpose for whatever you are going through.

Chapter 3

THE ORIGIN AND GENEALOGY OF THE CALL OF BARRENNESS

The call of barrenness began with Abraham and Sarah, however, let's see how it all began by taking a look at its origin. We see from scriptures that Abraham was from the lineage of Shem the first son of Noah. Noah had three sons, Shem, Ham and Japheth (Genesis 11:10-32). Shem was the only blessed son of Noah. Canaan the first son of Ham was cursed because of the sin of his father, who exposed Noah's nakedness to his brethren. As a result the entire lineage of Canaan was cursed. This curse was the reason why Abraham's lineage were not allowed to marry from Canaan. Japheth the third son of Noah on the other hand was destined to serve Shem.

Genesis 9:18. And the sons of Noah, that went forth of the ark, were Shem, and Ham, and Japheth: and Ham is the father of Canaan.
19. These are the three sons of Noah: and of them was the whole earth overspread.
20. And Noah began to be an husbandman, and he planted a vineyard:

21. *And he drank of the wine, and was drunken; and he was uncovered within his tent.*

22. *And **Ham, the father of Canaan, saw the nakedness of his father, and told his two brethren without.***

23. *And Shem and Japheth took a garment, and laid it upon both their shoulders, and went backward, and covered the nakedness of their father; and their faces were backward, and they saw not their father's nakedness.*

24. *And Noah awoke from his wine, and knew what his younger son had done unto him.*

25. ***And he said, Cursed be Canaan; a servant of servants shall he be unto his brethren.***

26. *And he said, **Blessed be the LORD God of Shem; and Canaan shall be his servant.***

27. *God shall enlarge Japheth, and he shall dwell in the tents of Shem; and Canaan shall be his servant.*

From the stories in scriptures, we see that the gene for kingly seeds and kingly wombs was possibly domiciled in the lineage of Terah, Abraham's father. Terah was of the lineage of Shem. Terah had three sons, Abraham, Nahor and Haran. Haran had three notable children (Milkah, Iscah and Lot) before he died. Nahor married Milkah his brother Haran's daughter and had eight children from her, and four from a concubine. One of Nahor's children from Milkah was Bethuel who gave birth to Rebecca (Isaac's wife), Laban and others. We see that Rebecca is Nahor's granddaughter, and by implication she is Abraham's grandniece. Rebecca's blood brother Laban is the father of Leah and Rachel, the wives of Jacob (Isaac's son). We see therefore that the kingly wombs and the kingly seeds were actually from the same kin.

It's important to note that of the three children of Terah, Abraham was chosen to carry the gene for the kingly seed while Sarah and Nahor were chosen to carry the gene for the kingly womb. In otherwords the gene for the kingly seed was domiciled in Abraham while that of the kingly womb was domiciled in Sarah and Nahor.

Historically, we see that the gene for the kingly wombs (the barren womb) was preserved through the lineage of Shem, Noah's first son, down to Terah and down to Sarah and Nahor, Abraham's brother. The women born through the lineage of Terah preserved the gene of the kingly (barren) womb. From scriptures we see that the kingly womb of Rebecca and Rachel was traceable to Nahor, Abraham's brother. Rebecca was Nahor's granddaughter and Rachel was Nahor's great granddaughter, and both were barren before bringing forth their children. The kingly womb found expression first in Sarah. From scriptures we see that Sarah was Abraham's half sister, she was the daughter of Terah. She had same father with Abraham but different mother.

Genesis 20:11. And Abraham said, Because I thought, Surely the fear of God is not in this place; and they will slay me for my wife's sake.
*12. And yet **indeed she is my sister; she is the daughter of my father, but not the daughter of my mother; and she became my wife.***

We see therefore, that from the inception of the call of barrenness, three generations (Abraham, Isaac, Jacob) successively inherited this calling. Also Sarah, Rebecca and Rachel for the women.

Note that, in Abraham's generation consanguineous marriages were allowed. Consanguineous marriage is the union between two individuals who are related as second cousins or closer.

We see that the successive generational transference of this call was made possible by marrying from a particular kin where this call was domiciled. Abraham understood this, such that when Isaac was ready for marriage he made sure that his servant swore to marry a wife for his son from his kindred.

Genesis 24:1. And Abraham was old, and well stricken in age: and the LORD had blessed Abraham in all things.
*2. And Abraham said unto his eldest servant of his house, that ruled over all that he had, **Put, I pray thee, thy hand under my thigh:***
*3. **And I will make thee swear by the LORD, the God of heaven, and the God of the earth, that thou shalt not take a wife unto my son of the daughters of the Canaanites, among whom I dwell:***
*4. But thou shalt **go unto my country, and to my kindred, and take a wife unto my son Isaac.***
7. The LORD God of heaven, which took me from my father's house, and from the land of my kindred, and which spake unto me, and that sware unto me, saying, Unto thy seed will I give this land; he shall send his angel before thee, and thou shalt take a wife unto my son from thence.
*15. And it came to pass, before he had done speaking, that, **behold, Rebekah came out, who was born to Bethuel, son of Milcah, the wife of Nahor, Abraham's brother**, with her pitcher upon her shoulder.*

Isaac also understood this and ensured that his son Jacob married from his kindred.

*Genesis 28:1. And Isaac called Jacob, and blessed him, and charged him, and said unto him, **Thou shalt not take a wife of the daughters of Canaan.***
*2. Arise, **go to Padan-aram, to the house of Bethuel thy mother's father; and take thee a wife from thence of the daughters of Laban thy mother's brother.***
3. And God Almighty bless thee, and make thee fruitful, and multiply thee, that thou mayest be a multitude of people;
*4. **And give thee the blessing of Abraham, to thee, and to thy seed with thee**; that thou mayest inherit the land wherein thou art a stranger, which God gave unto Abraham.*

It's important to note that what Abraham and Sarah (and their successive generations) were fulfilling was a call. It was not a mere inability to conceive children but a call to fulfil a purpose.

*Isaiah 51:1. Hearken to me, ye that follow after righteousness, ye that seek the LORD: **look unto the rock whence ye are hewn**, and to the hole of the pit whence ye are digged.*
*2. **Look unto Abraham your father, and unto Sarah that bare you: for I called him alone, and blessed him**, and increased him.*

Abraham and Sarah serve as a model for the call of barrenness. We are to learn from them, because everyone with the call of barrenness is hewn from Abraham, and came out of Sarah and must therefore follow the example of Abraham and Sarah.

ABRAHAM'S CIRCUMCISION AND THE PROMISED SEED

From scriptures we see that ALL men from the time of Cain down to the time of Abraham were born without circumcision and most of these men (like Enoch, Noah, Methuselah) were holy men used by God. But have you ever wondered why Abraham was asked by God to circumcise himself, his seed and his household? It's important to understand that God's covenant with Abraham was domiciled in Abraham's reproductive system, and that was why Abraham was asked to circumcise himself as a token of the covenant. Such that from the moment Abraham got circumcised he was to bring forth a unique breed of people. Note that only those who are circumcised can fulfil the call of barrenness. Here's what God said to Abraham.

Genesis 17:10. ***This is my covenant, which ye shall keep, between me and you and thy seed after thee; Every man child among you shall be circumcised.***
11. And ye shall circumcise the flesh of your foreskin; and ***it shall be a token of the covenant betwixt me and you.***

It was after Abraham was circumcised that he entered into the covenant. At Abraham's circumcision God did something to Abraham's reproductive gene that empowered his seed to become what God has promised. This gene was to be transferred from generation to generation and the channel for this transference was through his reproductive system.

Note that God's promise of fruitfulness to Abraham was a tripartite promise, that is, it was in three parts.
- *One, that He will make him exceeding fruitful;*
- *Two, that He shall make nations come out of him;*
- *Three, that kings shall come out of him.*

But for this to happen he had to prepare the tool for the fulfilment of this promise through circumcision.

Genesis 17:5. Neither shall thy name any more be called Abram, but thy name shall be Abraham; for a father of many nations have I made thee.
*6. And **I will make thee exceeding fruitful, and I will make nations of thee, and kings shall come out of thee.***

For the first part of being exceeding fruitful, we see that God has indeed made Abraham exceedingly fruitful. God has also made nations arise from Abraham. God has also made kings to come out of Abraham through Israel. However, as it concerns the kingly seeds there is also a spiritual kind of kings that were promised to arise from Abraham. These kings are not the earthly kind of kings but these are men that serve both as kings and as priests, their kingship transcends beyond the earthly realm, they are men of influence, power and authority, who have power and control over the earthly kings. This part of the covenant finds expression or fulfilment only in the first born male of Abraham's seed. I believe this was the reason God declared the first born children as his, because these are special children who bear the covenant.

Part of what Abraham did not know about this covenant (and which he didn't need to know) was that the promised seed would need a barren (kingly) womb to nourish it for it to be born. God insisted that the promised seed would come from Sarah who was barren at the time. Remember, that it was after Abraham's circumcision that he came into the covenant. The circumcision of Abraham imparted a special kingly nature on Abraham's seed. I believe at Abraham's circumcision God would have changed something in the genetic composition of Abraham that made his seed to become the special kingly seeds (possibly God tweaked Abraham's gene to enhance the ability of his seeds). After his circumcision Abraham's sperm cells (seeds) became the promised kingly seeds. Every seed that came from Abraham after his circumcision came into the covenant and inherited the genetic composition, which made it the promised kingly seed. But it's important to know however that **the kingly gene is dominant in the firstborn males and recessive in the other males**. These dominant and recessive kingly genes find phenotypic expressions depending on the allele present, in accordance with man's current genetic understanding.

Note however, that Ishmael was born thirteen years before the circumcision of Abraham so he did not inherit this special nature or gene from Abraham his father, because this special nature was imparted on Abraham at his circumcision. And that is why the descendants of Ishmael cannot have this call of barrenness because they did not inherit it from Abraham.

Today in science, through genome editing man can choose the genetic makeup of an individual by tweaking their DNA, thus producing humans who are immune to some diseases and enhanced in many ways. Today we have Lulu and Nana (nicknames) as products of this genome editing. If man can achieve this great feat by tweaking the human gene, then imagine what God the Maker of man can achieve when He edits or tweaks our gene.

It's important to note that, even though Abraham's sperm cells became kingly seeds after his circumcision, these seeds still need a kingly (barren) womb to bring forth the promised kingly seed. When this kingly sperm cells are released into an unkingly womb they become corrupted and loss their full capacity to bring forth the promised kingly child. This is similar to what happens in the genetic crossing of an AA genotype (healthy) with an SS genotype (sickle cell), which will alter the genetic composition of the healthy AA. What we know today through science is a picture of God the Designer's template of spiritual things.

THE CORRUPTION OF THE KINGLY SEEDS AND THE INTERRUPTION OF THE CALL OF BARRENNESS.

The inception of the call of barrenness began with Abraham after the circumcision where his reproductive gene was enhanced. The enhanced gene from Abraham was meant to be transferred from generation to generation such that from that time forth there should be the birth of this special breed of men in **every** generation. This design was however interrupted along the line by the corruption of the kingly seeds.

The call of barrenness was sustained for three generations after its inception through consanguineal marriage. The call was sustained from Abraham to Isaac and unto Jacob. However, the children of Jacob corrupted the seed and interrupted the call by marrying from other tribes outside their kin; especially tribes whose union with Israel was pernicious. We see from scriptures that most of the sons of Jacob (especially the ones who have the first born mantle, Reuben, Joseph and Judah) married from tribes other than their kin. Reuben married a Canaanite woman, Judah married a Canaanite woman and Joseph married an Egyptian. Reuben lost his place as first born to Joseph due to sexual misconduct, thus transferring the mantle of this call to Joseph.

*1 Chronicles 5:1. Now the sons of Reuben the firstborn of Israel, (for he was the firstborn; but, forasmuch as he defiled his father's bed, **his birthright was given unto the sons of Joseph the son of Israel: and the genealogy is not to be reckoned after the birthright.**
2. For Judah prevailed above his brethren, and of him came the chief ruler; but the birthright was Joseph's:)*

Joseph by virtue of his place as the first born son of Rachel and by virtue of the fact that he was born of a barren womb, did not only become the promised kingly offspring but he also became the custodian of the dominant kingly gene in his generation. The kingly gene was dominant in Joseph and was meant to find expression in his direct offspring if he married the right woman. However, Joseph's marriage to Asenath completely corrupted the seed and interrupted the transference of this call to the next generation. The effect of Asenath's womb was evident in the life of her children Ephraim and Manasseh.

This unholy union between Jacob's sons corrupted the kingly seeds and interrupted the call for many generations, some of which took up to thirty generations to purify. Even with the positive eugenics and genetic cleansing, yet it took many generations for most of the kingly gene to be purified and restored. The generations apart between Jacob to Samson, to Samuel and to John the Baptist will give you an idea of how many generations it took for most of the kingly genes to be purified and restored.

MARRIAGE AND THE KINGLY SEEDS

The emergence of the kingly children is highly dependent on the union of marriage. The choice of spouse in marriage determines the continuity of the call of barrenness. Getting married to the wrong person will affect the gene and interrupt the call. At the inception of the call of barrenness, consanguineal marriage was the only way through which the kingly seeds were born and through which the call was sustained. This is possibly because the gene for the kingly seed and kingly womb was localised in one family at the inception of the call. However, when the law came God prohibited consanguineal marriage, at this time the kingly gene had multiplied and spread beyond a kindred.

God had to ask Moses to write down the statutes on marriage to kin for them to observe.

Leviticus 18:1. And the LORD spake unto Moses, saying,
2. Speak unto the children of Israel, and say unto them, I am the LORD your God.
5. Ye shall therefore keep my statutes, and my judgments: which if a man do, he shall live in them: I am the LORD.

6. None of you shall approach to any that is near of kin to him, to uncover their nakedness: *I am the LORD.*

7. *The nakedness of thy father, or the nakedness of thy mother, shalt thou not uncover: she is thy mother; thou shalt not uncover her nakedness.*

8. *The nakedness of thy father's wife shalt thou not uncover: it is thy father's nakedness.*

9. *The nakedness of thy sister, the daughter of thy father, or daughter of thy mother, whether she be born at home, or born abroad, even their nakedness thou shalt not uncover.*

10. *The nakedness of thy son's daughter, or of thy daughter's daughter, even their nakedness thou shalt not uncover: for theirs is thine own nakedness.*

11. *The nakedness of thy father's wife's daughter, begotten of thy father, she is thy sister, thou shalt not uncover her nakedness.*

12. *Thou shalt not uncover the nakedness of thy father's sister: she is thy father's near kinswoman.*

13. *Thou shalt not uncover the nakedness of thy mother's sister: for she is thy mother's near kinswoman.*

14. *Thou shalt not uncover the nakedness of thy father's brother, thou shalt not approach to his wife: she is thine aunt.*

15. *Thou shalt not uncover the nakedness of thy daughter in law: she is thy son's wife; thou shalt not uncover her nakedness.*

16. *Thou shalt not uncover the nakedness of thy brother's wife: it is thy brother's nakedness.*

17. *Thou shalt not uncover the nakedness of a woman and her daughter, neither shalt thou take her son's daughter, or her daughter's daughter, to uncover her nakedness; for they are her near kinswomen: it is wickedness.*

After the law consanguineal marriage was no more necessary for the emergence of the kingly seeds, hence those with the call do not need to get married to their kin before they can fulfil the call. This is because the gene for the kingly seed as well as the kingly womb are no more localised in one family tree but have spread even beyond the tribe of Israel.

In our present day, it is difficult by our human effort to identify those who have this call; neither can we influence our choice of spouse in other to fulfil the call because humanly, this call can only be identified after marriage through barrenness. From the inception of the call up until now, God is the only matchmaker of those with the call, he chooses those he wants to fulfil this call, and hence we must depend on Him to direct our choices in marriage. No matter what we do we can never know if we have the call or not until we get married, neither can we know if the person we are getting married to has the call or not. And that is why as a couple, if you discover that you have this call upon your life, you should treasure it and work to sustain its continuity in your life and children. ***As a man if you discover that your wife is barren as a result of the call (or has a kingly womb), you should be super excited because your marriage is made in heaven.*** God would have supernaturally brought you together to fulfil this purpose/call.

The continuity of the kingly seeds and kingly wombs is highly dependent on marriage. Ezra the priest understood this and was greatly pained when he discovered that the children of Israel were having children with other tribes other than Israel. From scriptures, we see that even the priests, Levites and all the people of Israel knew that marriage to other tribes other than Israel would corrupt the kingly seed. In their report to Ezra they even referred to the kingly seed as a holy seed, which means they knew that in them was an holy (kingly) seed and that their marriage to the strange women had corrupted that holy seed.

Ezra 9:1. Now when these things were done, the princes came to me, saying, The people of Israel, and the priests, and the Levites, have not separated themselves from the people of the lands, doing according to their abominations, even of the Canaanites, the Hittites, the Perizzites, the Jebusites, the Ammonites, the Moabites, the Egyptians, and the Amorites.
*2. **For they have taken of their daughters for themselves, and for their sons: so that the HOLY SEED have mingled themselves with the people of those lands**: yea, the hand of the princes and rulers hath been chief in this trespass.*
*3. And **when I heard this thing, I rent my garment and my mantle, and plucked off the hair of my head and of my beard,** and sat down astonished.*

Whatever would make a man rend his garment, pluck off the hair of his head and beard must be something very serious. The children of Israel had committed many sins before now but this transgression of unholy marriage was difficult to bear because it concerns the pollution and endangerment of the kingly seed. This was an evil and a transgression that they needed to take immediate action if they must not be consumed by the wrath of God.

This unholy marriage to strange wives made God angry with the children of Israel. God was angry with the children of Israel because by getting married to the prohibited tribes they were polluting his kingly seed. It was so serious that in other to turn away the wrath of God from them the children of Israel who had married strange wives had to put the women away and separate themselves from them and even offer blood sacrifice for the atonement of their sin. The number of Israelites involved in this transgression was so great that it took three months (from the first day of the tenth month to the first day of the first month) to examine, identify and make atonement for all who had married strange wives. This I believe contributed to the cessation of the kingly seeds for many generations.

(Read the entire book of Ezra chapter nine and ten to understand the depth of the matter).

Almost all the sons of Jacob got married to strange women; they did not marry from their kin, which in turn imparted on their own offspring. The result of these strange marriages is the corruption of their kingly gene. Let's take a look at the children of Israel whose kingly gene managed to find expression in the future and how long it took, as documented in the bible.

LEVI TO ELKANAH TO SAMUEL

*1 Samuel 1:1. Now there was a certain man of Ramathaim-zophim, of mount Ephraim, and his name was **Elkanah**, the son of **Jeroham**, the son of **Elihu**, the son of Tohu, the son of Zuph, an Ephrathite:*
2. And he had two wives; the name of the one was Hannah,

and the name of the other Peninnah: and Peninnah had children, but Hannah had no children.
20. Wherefore it came to pass, when the time was come about after Hannah had conceived, that she bare a son, and called his name **Samuel***, saying, Because I have asked him of the LORD.*

Levi was Jacob's third son from Leah. By reason of his birth position the kingly gene in him became recessive. Which means that even if he had married the right woman with the kingly womb, his direct offspring will still not become the special kingly seed until after many generations of genetic crossing and purging.

Samuel was a Levite by descent, that is, he was a descendant of the tribe of Levi, Jacob's third son. In first Chronicles chapter six the lineage of Elkanah the father of Samuel could be traced to the tribe of Levi. Looking at the genealogy of Samuel it took about *ten generations from Jacob to Samuel.* In other words it took about ten generations for the kingly gene to be purified and to find expression. So for ten generations there was no manifestation of the kingly gene because of the wrong choice in marriage by Jacob's children.

Samuel on the other hand had two children who did not work in his ways but did evil in the sight of God. This could possibly be because of the tribe of the woman he married.

1 Samuel 8:1. And it came to pass, when Samuel was old, that he made his sons judges over Israel.
2. Now the name of his firstborn was Joel; and the name of

his second, Abiah: they were judges in Beer-sheba.
3. And his sons walked not in his ways, but turned aside after lucre, and took bribes, and perverted judgment.

DAN TO MANOAH TO SAMSON

*Judges 13:2. And there was a certain man of Zorah, of the family of the Danites, whose name was **Manoah**; and his wife was barren, and bare not.*
*24. And the woman bare a son, and called his name **Samson**: and the child grew, and the LORD blessed him.*
25. And the Spirit of the LORD began to move him at times in the camp of Dan between Zorah and Eshtaol.

Samson was the son of Manoah, a Danite. In otherwords, Samson was a descendant of Dan. Dan was Jacob's 5th son, and Bilhah's first child, which she bore to Jacob. Bilhah was Rachel's maid. She gave birth to Dan and Naphtali.

Genesis 30:1. And when Rachel saw that she bare Jacob no children, Rachel envied her sister; and said unto Jacob, Give me children, or else I die.
2. And Jacob's anger was kindled against Rachel: and he said, Am I in God's stead, who hath withheld from thee the fruit of the womb?
*3. And she said, **Behold my maid Bilhah, go in unto her;** and she shall bear upon my knees that I may also have children by her.*
*4. And **she gave him Bilhah her handmaid to wife: and Jacob went in unto her.***
*5. And **Bilhah conceived, and bare Jacob a son.***
6. And Rachel said, God hath judged me, and hath also heard

*my voice, and hath given me a son: therefore called **she his name Dan.***

Bilhah did not have a kingly womb so the union of her womb with Jacob's kingly seed could not produce the covenant seed. However Dan retained a recessive kingly gene, which was passed through many generations to become dominant in Manoah, who was blessed to marry a woman with the kingly womb. The union of Manoah's kingly gene with his wife's kingly womb brought forth Samson the special kingly priest. Dan could have married a woman without a kingly womb, which also affected the manifestation of the gene for many generations. It took over 470 years from Dan to Samson, in other words it took over 470 years for a kingly seed to come through the lineage of Dan.

JUDAH TO ZACHARIAS TO JOHN THE BAPTIST

*Luke 1:5. There was in the days of Herod, the king of Judaea, a certain priest named **Zacharias**, of the course of **Abia**: and his wife was of the daughters of **Aaron**, and her name was **Elisabeth**.*
7. And they had no child, because that Elisabeth was barren, and they both were now well stricken in years.

*Matthew 1:7. And Solomon begat Roboam; and Roboam begat **Abia**; and Abia begat Asa;*

Elisabeth was of the priestly lineage of Aaron, Moses blood brother. The mother of Moses and Aaron was Jochebed. Jochebed was the daughter of Levi, Jacob's third son. Their father was Amram who also was a Levite. Amram's father was Kohath (the second son of Levi). Interestingly, Jochebed is the sister to Kohath, which means Amram married his father's sister or aunt.

*Exodus 2:1. And there went **a man of the house of Levi, and took to wife a daughter of Levi.***
2. And the woman conceived, and bare a son: and when she saw him that he was a goodly child, she hid him three months.

Zacharias on the other hand was a descendant of Judah, the fourth son of Israel (Jacob). He is said to be from Abia, Abia is the son of Jeroboam (Jeroboam the son of Solomon).
About thirty-eight generations passed between the time of Judah to the time that John the Baptist was born. The precious kingly seed was undergoing genetic purification or purging within this period. It took this long possibly because of the woman Judah married.

Let's go back in history to take a look at Judah's marriage. Judah married a Canaanite woman Shuah who gave birth to his first son called Er. Judah married Tamar for his son Er. Er was wicked and God killed him and as such did not have a seed through Tamar. (The wickedness of Er could be as a result of the unholy union of Judah with the Canaanite woman, remember the children of Israel were warned not to marry from Canaan).
In other to sustain the seed of his first son, Judah asked his second son Onan to marry Tamar by way of a levirate union in other to have a child for Er. Onan performed *coitus interruptus,* spilling on the ground the precious sperm (kingly seed) that God had been watching over instead of in

Tamar's womb for a selfish reason and God killed him for that costly action. By this time Judah had lost his two sons and was left only with Shelah his third son who was still young at the time. Tamar, the young widow returned to her father's house at the instruction of Judah to remain a widow until Judah's third son Shelah is mature enough to marry her. This he did in other to avoid losing his third son Shelah the way he lost the second Onan.

In the process of time, Judah lost his wife and in a bid to overcome his grief he unknowingly slept with Tamar his first son's wife who disguised herself as a harlot. Tamar disguised herself to sleep with Judah because she saw that Shelah was grown and she was not given to him to marry. The union between Judah and Tamar brought forth twins (in a manner similar to the birth of Jacob and Esau), the first of which was Pharez.

Pharez by reason of his firstborn place became the custodian of the special kingly gene from this bloodline, however at this time the womb that bore him had corrupted the special gene and it had to take another thirty generations for it to be purified. Zacharia the father of John the Baptist was of the lineage of this Pharez.

*Genesis 38:2. And **Judah** saw there a daughter of a certain **Canaanite**, whose name was **Shuah**; and he took her, and went in unto her.*
*7. And **Er, Judah's firstborn, was wicked** in the sight of the LORD; and **the LORD slew him.***
29. And it came to pass, as he drew back his hand, that, behold, his brother came out: and she said, How hast thou

*broken forth? this breach be upon thee: therefore his name was called **Pharez**.*

(Read the full story in Genesis 38).

THE SPREADING ABROAD OF THE KINGLY SEEDS AND WOMBS TO OTHER NATIONS

Through the union of marriage the kingly gene has today spread beyond the land of Israel and many who are not Israelites by location have come to carry this gene such that after many generations the gene gets purified, become dominant and finds expression. And at the appointed time God brings a kingly womb to a holy union with the kingly seed. I believe God is watching to bring His promise to Abraham to pass. However, it's important to note that not all women have the kingly (barren) womb and as such the kingly womb now becomes the determinant factor for the precious kingly priests that should be born.

Today the kingly seeds and the kingly wombs have spread beyond Israel to other nations of the earth, even to the ends of the earth, to Africa, to Europe, to Asia, to America etc.

God had told the children of Israel that if they disobey his commandment and brake His covenant, as a punishment, He will scatter them among the heathen and from one end of the earth to another, to places where their father's have not known.

*Deuteronomy 28:64. And **the LORD shall scatter thee** among all people, **from the one end of the earth even unto the other**; and there thou shalt serve other gods, which neither thou nor thy fathers have known, even wood and stone.*

I believe this is what resulted in what is referred to today as the Lost Tribes of Israel. Today, populations from the *"Lost Tribes"* have been discovered in many places around the world, including Ethiopia, India, China, Zimbabwe, Afghanistan, Nigeria and other locations.

Please permit me to bore you a bit with this history. Back in history, in the time of Noah the entire continents were connected together, however five generations after Noah, in the time of Peleg, (the son of Eber, the son of Salah, the son of Arphaxad, the son of Shem, the son of Noah) the *continental drift* occurred, which divided the continent into their different continents. Before the continental drift man could travel from one nation or continent to another without going through the oceans, so it was easy for these different nations to travel intercontinentally. However with the passage of time the continents drifted away from each other.

*Genesis 10:25. And unto Eber were born two sons: the name of one was **Peleg; for in his days was the earth divided**; and his brother's name was Joktan.*

Science has helped us to understand what happened in the time of Peleg, scientists have discovered that tectonic plates movement caused this division of the earth. This movement causes the earth plates to move away from each other, and consequently causing the continents to drift apart. The rift between the splitting continents is what resulted in the Atlantic Ocean.

In the plate tectonic theory, it is believed that the continents move apart at the rate of *2.54cm/year (1inch/year)* and the drift could have taken about *250 million years* to get to its present state. In otherwords in the time of Abraham up to the time of Jacob and up to the time when Israel was scattered abroad (resulting in the lost tribe of Israel), the continents could still be close enough for easy intercontinental travels.

Due to the interconnection of these nations at that time, the children of Israel could travel to Egypt and other nations of the earth easily and intermarry with these nations thus spreading the kingly gene to these nations.

Note that Egyptians are the descendants of Ham, the son of Noah. And Ham was the father of Canaan. The land of Egypt is also known as the land of Ham. The following scriptures reveal this truth.

Psalm 78:51. And smote all the firstborn in Egypt; the chief of their strength in the tabernacles of Ham:

Psalm 105:23. **Israel also came into Egypt; and Jacob sojourned in the land of Ham.**
24. And he increased his people greatly; and made them stronger than their enemies.
26. He sent Moses his servant; and Aaron whom he had chosen.
27. They shewed his signs among them, and wonders in the

land of Ham.
28. He sent darkness, and made it dark; and they rebelled not against his word.
29. He turned their waters into blood, and slew their fish.
30. Their land brought forth frogs in abundance, in the chambers of their kings.
36. He smote also all the firstborn in their land, the chief of all their strength.

Psalm 106:21. They forgat God their saviour, which had done great things in Egypt;
22. Wondrous works in the land of Ham, and terrible things by the Red sea.

By reason of the sojourn of the children of Israel in Egypt and their intermarriage with the Egyptians the kingly seeds and kingly wombs could have been intermingled and transferred to the seeds from these intermarriages, thus spreading abroad (beyond Israel) the gene for the kingly seeds and the kingly wombs.

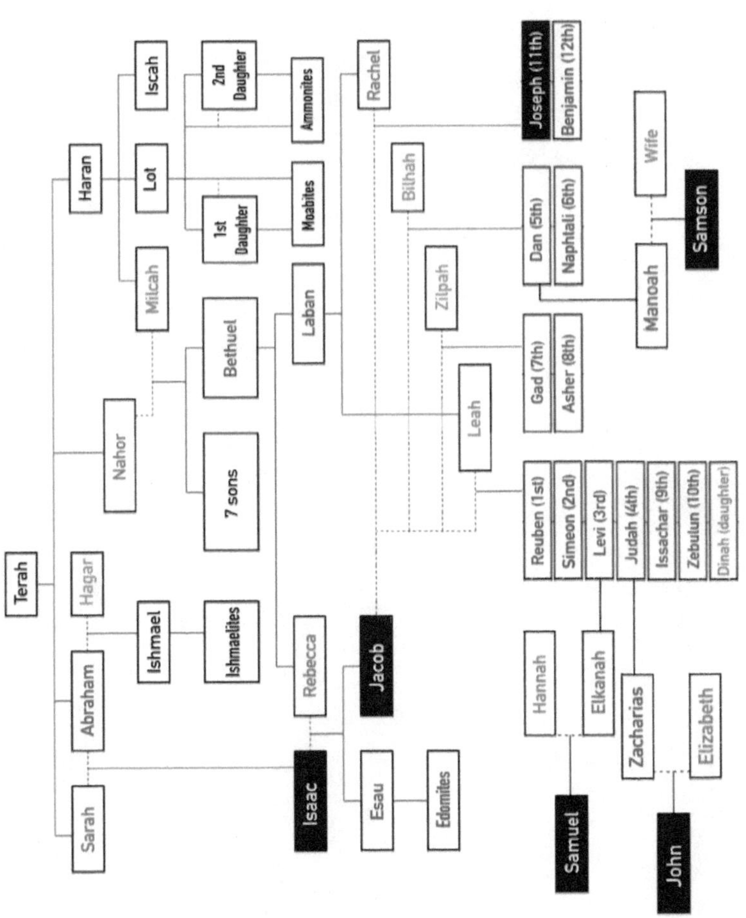

CHART SHOWING THE GENEALOGY OF THE KINGLY SEEDS

Chapter 4

The CALLED womb

The called womb is a barren womb that has a calling to bring forth a special breed of men who have a call of spiritual leadership to fulfil. This is a womb that has been touched and enhanced by God for the purpose of bearing a special breed of men who I refer to as kingly priests. I call this womb the kingly womb. Interestingly, barrenness is the identity of the called womb. It is the identity of those who have been ordained by God to carry the kingly priests promised Abraham. Barrenness is the identity of women who have kingly wombs. These kingly wombs are temporarily barren wombs.

These wombs are customised by God to be barren for an appointed time and to bear kingly children.

The called womb is a special and anointed womb, carefully, fearfully and masterly crafted by the Creator. These wombs are specially ordained to carry great men. Most great men in the biblical times were borne by a once barren womb.

Every *called* womb bears a child with a great call upon his life. This is evident in the life of all the products of the called wombs documented in the holy Bible, Isaac, Joseph, Jacob,

Samson, Samuel and John the Baptist. Let's see a practical example in the life of Jacob.

Isaiah 49:1. Listen, O isles, unto me; and hearken, ye people, from far; **The LORD hath called me from the womb***; from the bowels of my mother hath he made mention of my name.*
2. And he hath made my mouth like a sharp sword; in the shadow of his hand hath he hid me, and made me a polished shaft; in his quiver hath he hid me;
3. And said unto me, **Thou art my servant, O Israel***, in whom I will be* **glorified***.*
4. Then I said, I have laboured in vain, I have spent my strength for nought, and in vain: yet surely my judgment is with the LORD, and my work with my God.

The LORD hath called me from the womb...
Jacob was called right from his mother's womb. Remember he was a man born from a barren womb.

Thou art my servant, O Israel, in whom I will be glorified.
The story above is the story of Jacob as revealed to Isaiah. Remember Jacob is Israel. Looking at the story you will see how that Jacob was named or called by his name when he was in his mother's womb.

Then I said, I have laboured in vain, I have spent my strength for nought, and in vain: This is typical of the life of Jacob when Laban deceived him.

Isaiah 44:1. Yet now hear, **O Jacob my servant***; and Israel,* **whom I have chosen:**

2. Thus saith the LORD that made thee, and formed thee from the womb, which will help thee; Fear not, O Jacob, my servant; and thou, Jesurun, whom I have chosen.

We see from the above scriptures that Jacob was chosen from the womb to serve God.
Every called (barren) womb in the bible that eventually carried a child, carried a child of great destiny, no wonder the holy Bible says.

*Isaiah 54:1. **Sing, O barren**, thou that didst not bear; break forth into singing, and cry aloud, thou that didst not travail with child: for more are the children of the desolate than the children of the married wife, saith the LORD.*
*6. For **the LORD hath called** thee as a woman forsaken and grieved in spirit, and a wife of youth, when thou wast refused, saith thy God.*
7. For a small moment have I forsaken thee; but with great mercies will I gather thee.

The called wombs are not affected by menopause, they do not respond to biological timing, neither are they controlled or limited by the biological clock. These wombs conceive and bring forth children even after their climacteric years. These wombs are not controlled by natural phenomenon, they operate beyond the natural; they are supernatural.

Those with this call of barrenness should not be worried, anxious or concerned about menopause because post-menopausal childbirth is one characteristic feature and identity of this calling.

Those with this calling mostly bring forth their children after menopause, Yes! They hardly bring forth children before menopause. Note that most of the women (if not all) who had this calling in the Bible were very old or well stricken in age as the Bible puts it; Sarah (Genesis 18:11), Elizabeth, (Luke 1:7) etc. For Rachel and Rebecca we see that even if it was not recorded that they passed menopause, however we can easily deduce it from scriptures.

For Rachel, note that after her sister Leah had passed menopause, Leah's maid gave birth to two children for Jacob after which Leah herself later gave birth to three more children before Rachel finally put to birth her first child (Read Genesis 30). In other words after Leah's menopause five children were born successively before Rachel could have her first child. If these children were spaced one year apart, then five years would have elapsed. Which means Rachel could have also reached menopause before she put to birth her first child, considering that the age difference between Rachel and her sister Leah may not be up to ten years.

For Rebecca, we see that she put to birth her first child when her husband Isaac was 60 years old. Considering that Abraham his father was ten years older than Sarah (Genesis 17:17), if this also applied to Isaac and Rebecca then Rebecca could have also approached menopause at the time she put to birth her first child.

We see therefore that post-menopausal childbirth is a characteristic feature of the call of barrenness. It's important to note that the post-menopausal womb is the perfect womb for fulfilling the call of barrenness. Therefore for those who have this call, instead of getting anxious and worried when you approach menopause, rather get excited because you are approaching the peak and prime of your fruitfulness. Rejoice, because you are closer to the time of your bringing forth.

For those who do not have this calling the post-menopause years is their unproductive and unfruitful years. But for those with the calling of barrenness the post-menopausal years are their years of fruitfulness and productivity. Those with this calling should sensitively look out for these post-menopausal years for these are their years or season of fruitfulness.

Those with the call of barrenness must understand that they are not like other women, so they must not expect things to happen to them or work for them the way it happens to other women. The Lord Jesus gave this revelation about timing in the book of John seven verse six when he said to his brothers, ***"The right time for me has not yet come. Any time is right for you** (Good News Translation)"* when they asked Him to show Himself to the world that He can do miracles. In other words, He was saying by God's design according to His calling, He has a different timeline for the fulfilment of His purpose different from theirs. Based on our calling we have a different timeline for the fulfilment of our purpose, far different from that of others who do not have the same calling.

Beloved, there is an appointed time for our showing or manifestation according to our calling. We see that John the Baptist was not revealed to the people of Israel until the appointed time for his showing came (Luke 1:80). I strongly believe that if John were revealed before his time, he would have been killed earlier without having the opportunity to fulfil his purpose of baptising Jesus (John 1:31-34). Note that shortly after John the Baptist was shown to Israel at the instruction of God (Luke 3:2-3) and he baptised Jesus (and Jesus was driven into the wilderness for forty days), John was arrested and killed (Matthew 3:1-17, Matthew 4:1-10). Waiting for the appointed time for our showing or manifestation is very important for the fulfilment of our purpose and calling.

Our calling determines our time of showing. Those who are called to bring forth ordinary children have a different time of showing or timeline for bringing forth, different from those who are called to bring forth extraordinary children.
In God's timeline, the natural age for those without the calling to put to birth is before menopause while the natural age for those with the calling to put to birth or to be fruitful is after menopause.

I would therefore like to break this good news to you with joy in my heart that, ***"Your post menopausal age is your golden age". Your postmenopausal years are your years of fruitfulness.*** If you are reading this book and you have reached menopause without bringing forth a child, I congratulate you because you have entered your fruitful season. Get excited because you are in your golden age, you are in your fruitful season and hear this ***"no devil can stop your fruitfulness"***. Beloved of God, I rejoice with you. I celebrate you.

The called womb or the womb of purpose is like a fallow ground. And like every fallow ground the longer the land is left fallow the more fertile and enriched it becomes. The period from their birth to menopause is the fallow period. Like the product of every fallowed (enriched) earth, the product of this kind of (barren) womb is always better than others (which are not barren or left to fallow).

A called womb brings forth a called seed. Every first seed of a called womb is a called seed.

Romans 9:9. For this is the word of promise, At this time will I come, and Sara shall have a son.
10. And not only this; but when Rebecca also had conceived by one, even by our father Isaac;
*11. (For the children being not yet born, neither having done any good or evil, that **the purpose of God according to election might stand**, not of works, but of him that **calleth**;)*

I believe if a survey is conducted (in this present age) of men who were born from a once barren womb of faithful servants of God, these men would be seen to be among the most influential spiritual men of our time.

THE ROYALTY OF THE BARREN WOMB

There are **kingly wombs** and there are also **kingly seeds**. The kingly wombs are specially created for the kingly seeds. In our earthly tradition, there is a lineage and genealogy of kings; the same applies to God's kingdom on the earth.

In the earthly system, we see that specific families are seen as the royal family or the family of kings. In this royal setting we see that if you are not of the royal blood or royal family you cannot become a king. This goes to show that in the earthly system we recognise that there are wombs and seeds for kings. In other-words, there are kingly wombs and there are kingly seeds. Such that if you are not of the kingly womb or kingly seed you do not share in the royalty of that family.

In God's divine system we also see this distinction, such that we have special wombs for kings and special seeds for kings. These kings are not ordinary earthly kings but divinely ordained kings; the kingly priests. God specially made the seed of Abraham to be the seed of kings and Sarah's womb to be the womb for kings. To confirm this, God said to Abraham **"kings shall come out of thee and kings of people shall come out of Sarah"**.

Genesis 17:5. Neither shall thy name any more be called Abram, but thy name shall be Abraham; for a father of many nations have I made thee.
*6. And I will make thee exceeding fruitful, and I will make nations of thee, and **kings shall come out of thee**.*
15. And God said unto Abraham, As for Sarai thy wife, thou shalt not call her name Sarai, but Sarah shall her name be.
*16. And I will bless her, and give thee a son also of her: yea, I will bless her, and she shall be a mother of nations; **kings of people shall be of her**.*

When God said to Abraham **"kings shall come out of thee"**, He wasn't only saying it to Abraham, He was saying it to all who have the call of barrenness. Note that God said the same words to Jacob (Genesis 35:11), who was a direct seed of Isaac (the covenant seed of Abraham) and who himself had the call of barrenness.

Genesis 35:10. And God said unto him, Thy name is Jacob: thy name shall not be called any more Jacob, but Israel shall be thy name: and he called his name Israel.
11. And God said unto him, I am God Almighty: be fruitful and multiply; a nation and a company of nations shall be of thee, and ***"kings shall come out of thy loins".***

The barren womb is a womb specially created for divinely ordained kings. These kings are not crowned by man but by God therefore they may not walk around with physical crowns on their head. Their crown is a spiritual crown that sets them apart in life. The kingship of these kings is not like the earthly kingship that requires a throne, this kingship does not necessarily require a throne yet they have the same influence as an earthly king and even more. Isaac, Jacob, Joseph, Samson, Samuel and John all had the influence an earthly king would have.

There were many people in the time of Abraham including those with earthly kingship but none of them received the promise or prophecy of having kingly seeds, except Abraham and Sarah. It's important to note that in God's design there are special wombs for kings and there are also kingly seeds. Kings are not carried in ordinary wombs; kings are born by kingly wombs. It's also important to note that kingly wombs are especially designed for kingly seeds. And this kingly womb and kingly seed are identified through the call of barrenness. Abraham's seed was a kingly seed and Sarah's womb was a kingly womb, the kind the bible calls the royal priesthood. God could not let Abimelech to marry Sarah because her womb was for a kingly priest and Abimelech's seed (unlike Abraham's seed) was not the divinely ordained kingly seed. Bringing Abimelech's unkingly seed into Sarah's kingly womb would mesh up God's plan and covenant with Abraham. Have you ever wondered why God had to take it personal with Abimelech warning and threatening him with death if he goes ahead to marry Sarah? Have you ever thought that at that time many men would have been taking other men's wives yet God did not appear to them to warn and threaten them? Or perhaps you think it was because Abraham was a servant of God? Well, I believe God took it personal with Abimelech because He didn't want His plan, promise and covenant with Abraham to be thwarted.

Genesis 20:3. But God came to Abimelech in a dream by night, and said to him, Behold, thou art but a dead man, for the woman which thou hast taken; for she is a man's wife.
4. But Abimelech had not come near her: and he said, Lord, wilt thou slay also a righteous nation?
5. Said he not unto me, She is my sister? and she, even she herself said, He is my brother: in the integrity of my heart and innocency of my hands have I done this.
6. And God said unto him in a dream, Yea, I know that thou didst this in the integrity of thy heart; for I also withheld thee from sinning against me: therefore suffered I thee not to touch her.

Have you ever wondered why God would not allow the Israelites to marry from some tribes, especially the

Canaanites, Jebusites, Hivites, Amorites and Hittites etc? Because these people do not have a kingly womb otherwise known as the covenant or called womb and because their womb would corrupt the kingly seeds.

Deuteronomy 7:3. Neither shalt thou make marriages with them; **thy daughter thou shalt not give unto his son, nor his daughter shalt thou take unto thy son.**
4. For they will turn away thy son from following me, that they may serve other gods: so will the anger of the LORD be kindled against you, and destroy thee suddenly.
5. But thus shall ye deal with them; ye shall destroy their altars, and break down their images, and cut down their groves, and burn their graven images with fire.
6. For thou art an holy people unto the LORD thy God: the LORD thy God hath chosen thee to be a special people unto himself, above all people that are upon the face of the earth.

Prophet Nehemiah understood this mystery and when the children of Israel began to marry strange women from other tribes he resisted them and communing with God about it, he said, **"they have defiled the priesthood, and the covenant of the priesthood, and of the Levites".**

Nehemiah 13:25. And I contended with them, and cursed them, and smote certain of them, and plucked off their hair, and made them swear by God, saying, **Ye shall not give your daughters unto their sons, nor take their daughters unto your sons,** *or for yourselves.*
27. Shall we then hearken unto you to do all this great evil, to transgress against our God in marrying strange wives?
29. Remember them, O my God, because **they have defiled**

the priesthood, and the covenant of the priesthood, *and of the Levites.*

Bringing together in marriage a kingly womb and an unkingly seed or vice versa defiles the royal priesthood. The union between a kingly womb and an unkingly seed will produce a seed (or mixed breed) whose genetic composition will take many generations to clean up (or get rid of the defilement). This defilement is similar to what happens in the genetic composition of someone with SS genotype getting married to someone with AA genotype. This reduces the probability of having a purely royal priesthood seed to 50% through the seed of the mixed breed. As long as a seed with a mixed genetic composition is born, God's covenant with Abraham and the call of barrenness ceases. Until a pure breed is born after that unequal union, only then can the call of barrenness continue to be fulfilled.

Abraham's union with Sarah produced Isaac; Isaac and Rebecca's union produced Jacob. Jacob and Rachel's union produced Joseph. But Joseph missed it, through his marriage with the Egyptian Asenath, he disrupted the sequence of the flow of the call of barrenness from generation to generation. Joseph broke the sequence when He married Asenath, the daughter of the Pagan priest.

Genesis 41:45. And Pharaoh called Joseph's name Zaphnath-paaneah; and he gave him to wife Asenath the daughter of Poti-pherah priest of On. And Joseph went out over all the land of Egypt.

Asenath's womb was not a kingly womb and it corrupted Joseph's kingly seed. This I believe caused the call of barrenness to cease in Joseph's lineage. Note that all the women in the three generations before Joseph were barren, they had the call of barrenness, but Asenath did not, because of her lineage. Even though Joseph had the kingly seed yet Asenath's unkingly womb corrupted the seed and disrupted the sequence of transference of the call from Joseph's generation to the next generation.

Note that the children of Joseph, Ephraim and Manasseh by their father's unholy union became known for idolatry and all kinds of sexual immorality and whoredom.

Genesis 41:50. And unto Joseph were born two sons before the years of famine came, which Asenath the daughter of Poti-pherah priest of On bare unto him.
51. And Joseph called the name of the firstborn Manasseh: For God, said he, hath made me forget all my toil, and all my father's house.
52. And the name of the second called he Ephraim: For God hath caused me to be fruitful in the land of my affliction.

Hosea 4:17. Ephraim is joined to idols: let him alone.
18. Their drink is sour: they have committed whoredom continually: her rulers with shame do love, Give ye.

Hosea 5:3. I know Ephraim, and Israel is not hid from me: for now, O Ephraim, thou committest whoredom, and Israel is defiled.
4. They will not frame their doings to turn unto their God: for the spirit of whoredoms is in the midst of them, and they

have not known the LORD.

Hosea 12:1. Ephraim feedeth on wind, and followeth after the east wind: he daily increaseth lies and desolation; and they do make a covenant with the Assyrians, and oil is carried into Egypt.

Note that the grand design of bringing forth a male child as the first born in the call of barrenness was maintained in Joseph's seed (Manasseh) but because the seed was nourished by an idolatrous womb, the nature of the womb entered into the seed and corrupted the seed making the seed idolatrous by nature.
The unholy union between Joseph and Asenath did not only corrupt the seed but it also disrupted the flow of the call of barrenness from one generation to another, for many generations, such that in the bible it was not recorded if anyone from Joseph's lineage had the call. We know from scriptures however that the call was later seen in the lineage of Dan, Judah and Levi after many generations of genetic purification.

Note that the first born right was transferred from Manasseh to Ephraim by their grand father Israel. When Israel was blessing the children of Joseph before his death he put his right hand on Ephraim, thus putting Ephraim before Manasseh thereby making Ephraim the firstborn of Joseph (Genesis 48:17-20).

Now, see the spiritual mystery that happens when a kingly seed is unequally yoked with an unkingly womb, using Ephraim as our perfect example.

Hosea 9:10. I found Israel like grapes in the wilderness; I saw your fathers as the firstripe in the fig tree at her first time: but they went to Baal-peor, and separated themselves unto that shame; and their abominations were according as they loved.

*11. **As for Ephraim, their glory shall fly away like a bird, from the birth, and from the womb, and from the conception.***

12. Though they bring up their children, yet will I bereave them, that there shall not be a man left: yea, woe also to them when I depart from them!

*13. Ephraim, as I saw Tyrus, is planted in a pleasant place: but **Ephraim shall bring forth his children to the murderer.***

*14. Give them, O LORD: what wilt thou give? **give them a miscarrying womb and dry breasts.***

*16. Ephraim is smitten, **their root is dried up, they shall bear no fruit: yea, though they bring forth, yet will I slay even the beloved fruit of their womb.***

17. My God will cast them away, because they did not hearken unto him: and they shall be wanderers among the nations.

These are powerful words that affect the destiny of this seeds even before they are born. We see that the glory (power, authority and kingship) of the seed is lost even at conception as a result of the corruption of the unkingly womb. The moment the kingly seed enters the womb or fertilises the ovum, its glory departs: the glorious part of God in them that should make them godly and relevant in their time leaves them. This glory of the seed continues to depart from them while they are still in the womb and even at birth. Ah! My God! This mystery is so deep. The womb is such a powerful tool; it has the power to make a seed godly or to corrupt it. If we understand its power, we would understand why God warns against marrying from some tribes and we would be more careful in our choice of spouse.

Read more about Ephraim and you will see how God rejected this seed of Joseph, before in His infinite mercy He eventually showed him mercy.

THE BARREN WOMB CLOCK
(THE WOMB REGULATOR)

When God created the called womb, He created it specially such that no matter how such women try to get pregnant they cannot, because God the Creator has already tweaked the womb while creating it, to prevent child bearing until the appointed time.

The called barren womb is programmed by its Creator to act or function in a certain way that may not be medically discerned or understood. It's like putting an alarm on a clock, the alarm never rings until it's appointed time. God has the power to time the womb. He timed the womb to start releasing eggs and for menstruation to begin at an appointed time, He also timed the womb to shut down at an appointed time and medically we call it menopause. The same God who created the womb with such timing also has a way of timing the barren womb in a way that we may not understand.

From scriptures we see that God shuts and opens the womb for it to conceive and bear children (1 Samuel 1:5, Genesis 29:31, Genesis 30:22), that is what I call divine programming of the womb. The closing and opening of the womb is not a physically or medically controlled thing, it is a spiritual mystery. When God closes the womb, it doesn't mean He closes the cervix to prevent semen from going into the womb, semen would go into the womb but it will not have any fertilising effect on the womb. If the closing of the womb by God involves the closing of the cervix then such women would not be able to menstruate. Also the shutting of the womb does not mean that the egg in the women would not be released. The eggs would be released but it cannot be fertilised. What this simply means is that the reproductive system of the woman would function effectively but it has been spiritually tweaked or fine tuned to only conceive at an appointed time different from that of the normal womb. And that is why when such women go for medical examination; their reproductive system is usually seen to function effectively. This shows that the closing of the womb is simply a spiritual thing. It is more of a spiritual timing, just as we have physical timing, natural timing, we also have spiritual timing. The called womb is more or less being regulated by a spiritual timer.

HERALDING THE APPOINTED TIME OF LIFE

Heaven is conscious about time, it watches over time, and it never misses an appointed time. God tied everything he made on earth to time and that was why he created time first before creating any other thing. When God separated day and night it was time He created. And that is why there is time for everything under the heaven. Everything under heaven is controlled by time; it is only heaven that is not controlled by time.

Ecclesiastes 3:1. To every thing there is a season, and a time to every purpose under the heaven:
2. A time to be born, and a time to die; a time to plant, and a time to pluck up that which is planted;

Everything on the earth is tied to time including our purpose and calling. Every purpose on earth, including the purpose of barrenness is tied to time. There is a time to be born. There is an appointed time for the natural seeds to be born; there is also an appointed time for the called (kingly) seeds to be born. Interestingly, for the called seeds there is often a heralding before their arrival.

In God's blueprint for man, there is an appointed time of life for those with the call of barrenness different from that of those without the call. Their time to bring forth children is different from that of others.

Genesis 18:14. Is any thing too hard for the LORD? **At the time appointed I will return unto thee,** *according to the time of life,* **and Sarah shall have a son.**

And for those with the call of barrenness, God has a system of heralding the arrival of the seed. This could be by angelic visitation, by stirring up our spirit in the right direction or through dreams and visions.

When the appointed time comes for the barren to bring forth, there will be a stirring up in their spirit to pray the right prayer and to do that which they ought to do before they bring forth. There will be a kind of spiritual signal in their spirit that will stir them up in the right direction, more like a divine troubling, burden or disturbance in their spirit. Hannah had been going to Shiloh for many years but at the Shiloh where her prayer was answered, she had a burden in her heart. She became sorrowful and drunk in the Spirit. I believe that was a divine burden that was laid on her to herald the arrival of the precious seed, Samuel.

It was not a coincidence that before the arrival of Isaac the Godhead came to visit Abraham. The Godhead came in the bodily form of three men to visit Abraham and to announce the arrival of Isaac. It was not a coincidence that God came to visit Abraham a year before Sarah could bring forth, God came to stir up their spirit and prepare them for the arrival of the precious seed.

The angel that came to Manoah and Zechariah all came for the same purpose, to herald the arrival of Samson and John the Baptist. It was not a coincidence; it was a divine template for the spiritual awakening and preparation of the parents.

We must be sensitive to this divine signal and make the most of it. Abraham, Elkanah and all the men with this call knew their wife after the stirring up and they conceived.

To reveal the importance of this heralding, God the Father, God the Son and God the Holy Spirit had to came to

Abraham to stir him up and prepare him for the arrival of Isaac. This was necessary because often we loose hope on God's promises. Sarah had lost hope of ever conceiving but the arrival of the Godhead stirred up her hope and faith in preparation for the arrival of Isaac. Sarah in her heart had laughed and said how can I have a child now that I am so old.

God in one way or the other heralded the arrival of almost all the called seeds, He is the same God and He will do it for you. Therefore be expectant of God's visitation to herald the arrival of the precious kingly seed.

I am not a woman and I do not know what it feels like to be a woman but by divine inspiration I strongly feel that when the spiritual timer rings, the barren woman either naturally feels or spiritually discerns that it is her appointed time. There is always a herald or announcement of the appointed time. The appointed time for Sarah was announced (Genesis 18:14), that of Manoah was also announced (Judges 13:3), and also Elisabeth (Luke 1:13) etc.

This herald of the appointed time is what I believe is revealed in Isaiah 54.

Isaiah 54:1. Sing, O barren, thou that didst not bear; break forth into singing, and cry aloud, thou that didst not travail with child: for more are the children of the desolate than the children of the married wife, saith the LORD.
2. Enlarge the place of thy tent, and let them stretch forth the curtains of thine habitations: spare not, lengthen thy cords, and strengthen thy stakes;

3. For thou shalt break forth on the right hand and on the left; and **thy seed shall inherit the Gentiles, and make the desolate cities to be inhabited.**
6. For the LORD hath called thee as a woman forsaken and grieved in spirit, and a wife of youth, when thou wast refused, saith thy God.
7. For a small moment have I forsaken thee; but with great mercies will I gather thee.
13. And all thy children shall be taught of the LORD; and great shall be the peace of thy children.

When the appointed time is spiritually discerned the woman naturally or by impulse becomes joyful and begins to enlarge her tent and begins to make preparations for the arrival of the long awaited special breed of man sent to the earth to bless mankind.

Beloved, at your appointed time, you will discern and you will take the necessary steps.

Chapter 5

THE SPECIAL KINGLY SEED

*Genesis 17:16. And I will bless her, and give thee a son also of her: yea, I will bless her, and **she shall be a mother of nations; kings of people shall be of her.***

The seed or products of the called barren womb are ordained as kings from the womb. God speaking concerning Sarah said, she shall give birth to kings – a pointer to the great destiny of these special seeds. Kings are leaders and rulers of nations, they are men of sovereign power and authority; they are men of influence, distinction and capacity. They are men with God ordained leadership mantle upon them.

When God said concerning Sarah *"kings of people shall be of her"*, He wasn't only speaking about Sarah, He was also referring to all who have the call of barrenness as Sarah. And when He said to Abraham kings shall come out of thee, He was not only referring to Abraham but also unto the seeds of Abraham who have the same calling as him.

Note that the covenant God made with Abraham was not just with him but also with his seeds after him.

Genesis 17:4. As for me, behold, my covenant is with thee, and thou shalt be a father of many nations.

*6. And I will make thee exceeding fruitful, and I will make nations of thee, and **kings shall come out of thee.***

*7. And **I will establish my covenant between me and thee and thy seed after thee in their generations for an everlasting covenant**, to be a God unto thee, and to thy seed after thee.*

9. And God said unto Abraham, Thou shalt keep my covenant therefore, thou, and thy seed after thee in their generations.

10. This is my covenant, which ye shall keep, between me and you and thy seed after thee; Every man child among you shall be circumcised.

11. And ye shall circumcise the flesh of your foreskin; and it shall be a token of the covenant betwixt me and you.

As long as you are circumcised as a child of God and you circumcise your male children, you are baptised into that same covenant that God made with Abraham. Circumcision is the token of our acceptance and obedience to the covenant. Circumcision is an initiation into this old trans-generational covenant, it baptises the called into the covenant of fruitfulness. Have you ever wondered why to fulfil the covenant for fruitfulness, God asked Abraham to initiate circumcision? Have you ever wondered why it had to do with the instrument for man's fruitfulness?

Did you know that Abraham was not circumcised when he conceived Ishmael (Genesis 17:23-27)? Which means that at that time, he was not yet baptised or initiated into the covenant. Abraham's circumcision brought him into the covenant. Every seed Abraham had after his circumcision became a part of the trans-generational covenant. Note that Ishmael was not taken as the covenant seed, not because his mother Hagar was not Abraham's legitimate wife but because Abraham was not circumcised when he conceived Ishmael. It's important to note that Ishmael was a product of fleshly desires while Isaac was a product of the covenant or promise. And this distinction is the reason why, No descendant of Ishmael can have the call of barrenness, anyone from the descendants of Ishmael that is barren is not barren because they have the call of barrenness.

Let's see what the Holy Scriptures says concerning this.

*Hebrews 11:18. Of whom it was said, That **in Isaac shall thy seed be called:***

*Romans 9:7. **Neither, because they are the seed of Abraham, are they all children:** but, **In Isaac shall thy seed be called.***
*8. That is, They which are the children of the flesh, these are not the children of God: but **the children of the promise are counted for the seed.***
*9. For **this is the word of promise, At this time will I come, and Sara shall have a son.***
10. And not only this; but when Rebecca also had conceived by one, even by our father Isaac;
*11. (For the children being not yet born, neither having done any good or evil, **that the purpose of God according to election might stand,** not of works, **but of him that calleth;)***

However, this does not mean that the descendants of Ishmael cannot have another call; they can but certainly not the call of barrenness. There are many other calling that God can call the descendants of Ishmael to fulfil but just like the Levites have a unique calling, the call of barrenness is unique to the descendants of Isaac.

Unless perhaps, the descendant of Ishmael converts to Christ, only then can they receive this kind of calling.

Galatians 3:29. And if ye be Christ's, then are ye Abraham's seed, and heirs according to the promise.

Those who have this calling or who the covenant of the kingly seeds works for are those who are from the lineage of Isaac. Note that Manoah the father of Samson was a Danite, that is, a descendant of Dan. Dan was one of the sons of Jacob from Bilhah, Rachel's maid. The same relationship Hagar had with Abraham was the same Bilhah had with Jacob. However we see that Dan inherited the kingly gene while Ishmael did not. Circumcision made the difference for them to be brought into the covenant. Ishmael was born before the circumcision while Dan was born after the circumcision; hence he inherited the kingly gene. The kingly gene Dan inherited was what was passed through to Samson.

Of all of Abraham's children none made much impact as Isaac. Also of all of Jacob's children none made as much impact as Joseph. Jacob had other sons like Reuben, Simeon, Levi, Judah, Dan, Naphtali, Gad, Asher, Issachar, Zebulun etc. with other women who were not from the covenant womb of Rachel, and none of them made as much impact as Joseph, who was the first born of the covenant womb of

Rachel. In truth, all the brothers of Joseph depended on him for their livelihood at some point in their life.

I believe the dream of Joseph is a reflection of how that the seed from the covenant or barren womb is distinguished among other children from the same father who are not from the covenant womb.

Genesis 37:5. And Joseph dreamed a dream, and he told it his brethren: and they hated him yet the more.
7. For, behold, we were binding sheaves in the field, and, lo, **my sheaf arose, and also stood upright***; and, behold,* **your sheaves stood round about, and made obeisance to my sheaf.**
8. And his brethren said to him, **Shalt thou indeed reign over us? or shalt thou indeed have dominion over us?** *And they hated him yet the more for his dreams, and for his words.*
9. **And he dreamed yet another dream***, and told it his brethren, and said, Behold, I have dreamed a dream more; and,* **behold, the sun and the moon and the eleven stars made obeisance to me.**
10. And he told it to his father, and to his brethren: and his father rebuked him, and said unto him, What is this dream that thou hast dreamed? Shall I and thy mother and thy brethren indeed come to bow down ourselves to thee to the earth?

Joseph having the same dream twice was a confirmation to the truth that the destiny of this special breed of men is a destiny of leadership. Note that God used earthly witnesses (sheaves) and heavenly witness (the sun, moon and stars) to confirm the authority and influence of this special breed of men, signifying that heaven and earth would hold these men in high esteem. These special breeds of men are destined to be influential men in their time.

Rejecting, resisting or hating the destiny of these special breed of men does not stop their destiny from coming to pass, rather it facilitates it. Joseph's brethren resisted the destiny of Joseph but instead of stopping it, their resistance rather brought Joseph to the place where his destiny was to be fulfilled, thus facilitating the fulfilment of his glorious destiny. The more the destiny of this special breed of men is hated and resisted, the more their glorious destinies are fulfilled.

The seed from the once barren wombs may not have the same kind of dream that Joseph had, that is, their destiny may not be revealed to them the same way it was revealed to Joseph but that doesn't change the truth that they have the same kind of vision and purpose that Joseph had. In truth, they do not have to see the kind of dream Joseph saw in other to validate their mission, purpose or destiny. Those born in our contemporary time have the same heritage of leadership as those in the biblical time, their destiny may not be revealed as it was revealed to Joseph and others, nevertheless, they have the same glorious destiny as those in the biblical time.

The following must be noted about this breed of children.

1. They are the first born of the barren woman.
2. They are usually male children. (Note that most barren women in the bible whom God opened their womb gave birth to male children).
3. They are men of purpose.
4. They are influential men.
5. They are born spiritual leaders.
6. They stand out in their generation.

THE FIRSTBORN MALE

The firstborn male are very important to God because they are often used by God to bring to pass His special plan and purpose for mankind. The firstborn males by God's design are successors of kings, keepers of thrones, inheritors of power, kingdoms and dominion. They are the only ones chosen by God to fulfil the call of barrenness. God has special interest on firstborn children and that is why He asked that all the firstborn of Israel be separated and dedicated to Him. By God's design all firstborns belong to Him.

Exodus 13:1. And the LORD spake unto Moses, saying,
2. Sanctify unto me all the firstborn, whatsoever openeth the womb among the children of Israel, both of man and of beast: it is mine.

When God wanted to deliver Israel from the bondage of Egypt, we see God referring to Israel as His firstborn son.

The unwillingness of Pharaoh to release God's firstborn to Him moved God to kill the firstborn sons of Pharaoh. God needed His firstborn released from captivity so that they can continue to fulfil their call.

Note however, that every firstborn male must be brought into the covenant by circumcision. It's also important to note that what moved God to come for the rescue of the children of Israel in Egypt was his covenant of fruitfulness to Abraham, Isaac and Jacob. And remember that this covenant was a trans-generational covenant (Genesis 17:9) and the token for this covenant was the circumcision of the male children.

Exodus 2:23. And it came to pass in process of time, that the king of Egypt died: and the children of Israel sighed by reason of the bondage, and they cried, and their cry came up unto God by reason of the bondage.
*24. And God heard their groaning, and **God remembered his covenant with Abraham, with Isaac, and with Jacob.***
25. And God looked upon the children of Israel, and God had respect unto them.

Moses almost lost the life of his firstborn because he was not circumcised. When God said He would kill the firstborn sons of Pharaoh and the Egyptians, God would have also killed the firstborn son of Moses because he was not circumcised. This points to the truth that we cannot fulfil God's call with disobedience. Even though Moses was the one chosen by God to bring Israel out of bondage, yet God would have killed him if he didn't obey his instruction.

Exodus 4:22. And thou shalt say unto Pharaoh, Thus saith the LORD, Israel is my son, even my firstborn:
23. And I say unto thee, Let my son go, that he may serve me: and if thou refuse to let him go, behold, I will slay thy son, even thy firstborn.
24. And it came to pass by the way in the inn, that the LORD met him, and sought to kill him.
25. Then Zipporah took a sharp stone, and cut off the foreskin of her son, and cast it at his feet, and said, Surely a bloody husband art thou to me.
26. So he let him go: then she said, A bloody husband thou art, because of the circumcision.

One question comes to mind, why would God want to kill Moses? A man he has prepared from birth to save the children of Israel from bondage, after spending all this years to nurture Moses to this point. I begin to imagine, one moment God calls Moses to deliver Israel out of bondage, the next moment God wants to kill him. There must be something very important about this circumcision that would make God want to kill a man he has chosen and prepared over the years to fulfil such an important assignment.

I see that Moses disobedience to circumcise his sons was capable of jeopardising the entire mission hence it was better that it was fixed before the mission ever started. Imagine if Gershom, Moses firstborn son was killed alongside the firstborn of the Egyptians because he was not circumcised? I perceive that circumcision was the marker for differentiating the firstborn sons of Israel from those of the Egyptians. Moses and Zipporah his wife didn't understand that they were on a mission that could kill their own son, neither did they understand that the circumcision was for the security of their son, hence God had to find a way to enforce it, because He would not want to loose the firstborn son of His people, who also happen to belong to Him.

From the scriptures we see that Moses and Zipporah knew the reason why God wanted to kill Moses. Zipporah's reaction after she circumcised her son shows that she must have opposed it, which probably was because she did not follow the Abrahamic covenant of circumcision. And Moses on the other hand failed to circumcise his son due to her objection to the practice. This event at the Inn shows us how God takes seriously our commitment to his covenant.
In fulfilling our calling, we must weigh ourselves on the scale to be sure that our position does not stand in God's way or jeopardise God's plan and purpose.

The firstborn males belong to God and must be totally surrendered and dedicated to Him. Those with this calling must understand this truth and ensure they dedicate their firstborn sons to God. The truth is every firstborn son that is not dedicated to God becomes open for the devil to take. We see this truth manifest in the very firstborn son of mankind, Cain. Only God can secure the destiny of the firstborn from the pollution of the devil, hence they must be handed over to God. The devil is a destroyer of firstborns, to prevent him from touching the firstborn, we must hand them over to God, we must consecrate them to God. Moses while in the wilderness, in other to prevent the devil from destroying the firstborns, would always sprinkle blood on the children of Israel. He knew that the devil was after the firstborn.

*Hebrews 11:28. Through faith he kept the passover, and the **sprinkling of blood, lest he that destroyed the firstborn should touch them.***

We must not allow the devil to touch the firstborn of God, we must hastily consecrate them unto God to secure them for the fulfilment of their glorious destiny. When God is in control of the destiny of the firstborn, He makes them higher than the kings of the earth.

Psalm 89:27. Also I will make him my firstborn, higher than the kings of the earth.

This is God's plan for every firstborn male with the call of barrenness. It is for Him to exalt them higher than the kings of the earth and to establish their dominion and authority beyond that of the earthly kings (Presidents, Governors, Prime ministers etc).

SPIRITUAL ATTRIBUTES OF THE CALLED SEED

1. THEY ARE PRINCIPALITIES WHO HAVE THE AUTHORITY OF ARCHANGELS

The word principality is a derivative of a prince. A prince is a male ruler or head of a principality, territory, nation or kingdom. Jacob was a principality. He took authority over a territory at Penuel when he wrestled with the angel in prayer.

*Genesis 32:24. And Jacob was left alone; and there **wrestled a man** with him until the breaking of the day.*

25. And when he saw that he prevailed not against him, he touched the hollow of his thigh; and the hollow of Jacob's thigh was out of joint, as he wrestled with him.
26. And he said, Let me go, for the day breaketh. And he said, I will not let thee go, except thou bless me.
27. And he said unto him, What is thy name? And he said, Jacob.
28. And he said, Thy name shall be called no more Jacob, but Israel: **for as a prince hast thou power with God and with men, and hast prevailed.**

The angel Jacob fought with was a territorial angel who was the ruler over that territory. In the realm of the spirit, there are territorial angels of God and also territorial demonic angels or territorial demons. The territorial demons hinder the physical and spiritual advancement of people in a territory while the holy territorial angels promote and ensure the advancement of people in a territory. These territorial demons are named according to the territories they command. The princes of Persia and Grecia reflects the territory that they control as documented in Daniel 10:20.

When the angel called Jacob a prince, he was not referring to an earthly princehood but to a spiritual princehood, a principality. Jacob was a territorial power and commander. Remember the prince of Persia in the book of Daniel? The prince of Persia was a principality, such principalities are demonic territorial commanders that have authority and control over territories, kingdoms, nations, cities etc. such that for any man to exercise authority over that land they must first overcome the principalities of the land. The wrestling between Jacob and the angel was more like the wrestling between the prince of Persia and the angel sent to Daniel. This was what Paul by divine inspiration revealed that, we wrestle against principalities, powers and rulers of the darkness of this world (Ephesians 6:12). The prince of Persia fought the angel sent to Daniel for twenty-one days without victory but Jacob fought this angel in one night and overcame the angel. And the angel left Jacob with this testimony *"for as a prince (principality) hast thou power with God and with men, and hast prevailed".* At this point Jacob spiritually became a principality, a territorial commander, a gatekeeper, an authority, an overseer and a watcher over the nation of Israel.

Jacobs level of authority is of the order of archangel Michael. We see from scriptures that Angel Michael was identified as a prince in Daniel 10:21. It took the authority of angel Michael for the prince of Persia to be defeated. Any authority less than that of the class of angel Michael will not be able to defeat these territorial principalities.

These men have the power and authority of archangels. When they speak for the release of any captive soul or for the blessing of anyone, the prince of the land submits and obeys without delay. The principalities of the land are at their command. They submit to them because of their level of authority.

2. THEY ARE MEDIATORS BETWEEN GOD AND MAN

These are men that have been given the power and authority to defend nations before God. These are they that was spoken of by God when He said, *"I sought for a man*

among them, that should make up the hedge, and stand in the gap before me for the land, that I should not destroy it: but I found none. Therefore have I poured out mine indignation upon them; I have consumed them with the fire of my wrath: their own way have I recompensed upon their heads, saith the Lord GOD" (Ezekiel 22:30-31). God ordained these men to be in every generation to stand as mediators between God and man. Abraham in his time stood as a mediator between God and man, when he negotiated and mediated for the deliverance of Sodom from the wrath of God (Genesis 18:23-33). John the Baptist stood as a mediator between God and man to prevent the wrath of God from coming upon mankind. Speaking about John the Baptist, the holy bible says, **"Behold, I will send you Elijah the prophet before the coming of the great and dreadful day of the LORD: And he shall turn the heart of the fathers to the children, and the heart of the children to their fathers, lest I come and smite the earth with a curse"** (Malachi 4:5-6).

3. THEY ARE INTERCESSORS FOR NATIONS

These are men who by the Creators design have an intercessors grace to pray for the salvation and safety of nations. These are men of altars. They are men that know and understand how to raise prayer altars.

These men have the power to intercede for nations as evident in Abraham, Jacob, and Samuel etc. They have the power to bring nations out of the captivity of the principalities and powers of darkness and out of imminent damnation and judgement. Abraham negotiated with God for the salvation of Sodom. Jacob fought for the establishment and deliverance of the nation of Israel.

These men have the power to stop impending evil that has been ordained or decided in the realm of the spirit against nations. Joseph delivered nations out of the hunger and starvation that had already been decided in the realm of the spirit. Jacob fought with the angel that was resisting the advancement of Israel and took the key and authority of the heavens over the land; no wonder when he met Esau the anger of Esau was stayed. This I believe was because the demonic principalities that were stirring up Esau's anger against his brother were defeated at Penuel.

4. THEY HAVE A COVENANT OF ANSWERED PRAYERS WITH GOD.

These man have a covenant of answered prayers with God, whenever they call, God answers them. We see from scriptures that all the kingly seeds got instant answer to their prayers whenever they prayed. As soon as Isaac entreated God for his wife, God answered him. As soon as Samson prayed for the restoration of his strength God answered him. When Jacob prayed to God for a change of story from a man to a prince (for the conferment of the dominion of a principality), even when it was a difficult thing to ask yet his prayers got answered. All these are proofs that they have a covenant of answered prayers with God.

Genesis 25:21. And Isaac intreated the LORD for his wife, because she was barren: and the LORD was intreated of him, and Rebekah his wife conceived.

Judges 16:28. And Samson called unto the LORD, and said, O Lord GOD, remember me, I pray thee, and strengthen me, I pray thee, only this once, O God, that I may be at once avenged of the Philistines for my two eyes.

5. THEY ARE SEERS (PROPHETS)

These men are seers. They have an unusual power of foresight. They have the power to see into the future. Seers are prophets. They are prophets who have the authority to divine the future, communicate and receive instructions directly from God.

1 Samuel 9:9. (Beforetime in Israel, when a man went to inquire of God, thus he spake, Come, and let us go to the seer: for he that is now called a Prophet was beforetime called a Seer.)
19. And Samuel answered Saul, and said, I am the seer: go up before me unto the high place; for ye shall eat with me to day, and to morrow I will let thee go, and will tell thee all that is in thine heart.

Beginning with Abraham, Abraham was a seer, he could see God and Angels as if in the natural realm. God Himself approved Abraham as a prophet when He said to Abimelech, **"Restore the man his wife; for he is a prophet, and he shall pray for thee, and thou shalt live:"** (Genesis 20:7).

Jacob was a seer; through the power of foresight he was able to produce a rare breed of animals (Genesis 31:10-13). He saw God's plan ahead of time and received divine instruction directly from God. Joseph could see and tell the future through dreams. Samuel was a seer, as well as John the Baptist.

In closing this chapter, it is important to note that, this special breed of men may encounter various challenges in the course of fulfilling their divine leadership purpose, nevertheless they will fulfil their purpose at the appointed time. This understanding will help all those with this purpose and calling to be assured of the fulfilment of their purpose despite the challenges. Isaac, Jacob, Joseph, Samuel, Samson, John were all faced with one challenge or the other, nevertheless they fulfilled their purposes despite the challenges.

Its also important to note that, all these men though supernaturally ordained from the womb to fulfil a great purpose yet being in the flesh they have their weaknesses and are faced with the same challenge of the flesh and the world to contend with, as every other human. Samson for instance had the weakness of the lust of the flesh. Jacob had the weakness of deceit caused by the pride of life. These great men must therefore watch against limiting forces that manifest through the flesh and the world.

THE KINGLY SEEDS AND ALCOHOL

Most of the kingly seeds are called to be Nazarites and part of the Nazarite vow is that they must not drink alcohol or any kind of wine. From scriptures, we see that the kingly seeds like Samuel, Samson and John were asked not to drink wine as a result of their calling.

Let's see what is written about kings and alcohol in the Holy Scriptures.

*Proverbs 31:1. The words of king Lemuel, the **prophecy** that his mother taught him.*
*2. What, my son? and what, the son of my womb? and what, the **son of my vows**?*
3. Give not thy strength unto women, nor thy ways to that which destroyeth kings.
*4. **It is not for kings, O Lemuel, it is not for kings to drink wine; nor for princes strong drink:***
5. Lest they drink, and forget the law, and pervert the judgment of any of the afflicted.
6. Give strong drink unto him that is ready to perish, and wine unto those that be of heavy hearts.
7. Let him drink, and forget his poverty, and remember his misery no more.

The above scripture is a prophecy given to a king called Lemuel by his mother. The identity of Lemuel and his mother was not clearly defined in scriptures. Theologians and bible scholars are at variance on the identity of the two very important personalities spoken of in the aforementioned scripture. However, I strongly believe that king Lemuel refers to the kingly seeds and that this reference was made directly to Samuel by his mother Hannah. Lemuel means *belonging to God* or *dedicated to God*. Lemuel was the son of a vow made. From scriptures we see that Hannah made a vow to God, which brought forth Samuel. Samuel was a son of the vow Hannah made to God after which she dedicated the child to God.

*1 Samuel 1:11. And **she vowed a vow,** and said, O LORD of hosts, if thou wilt indeed look on the affliction of thine handmaid, and remember me, and not forget thine handmaid, but wilt give unto thine handmaid a man child, then **I will give him unto the LORD all the days of his life, and there shall no rasor come upon his head**.*

We also see that when Hannah was praying for Samuel after she handed him over to God she referred to him as a king. Hannah in her prayer and prophecy upon Samuel was prophesying using spiritual vocabulary. In the realm of the spirit the kingly seeds are seen as kings and Hannah understood this mystery very well hence she was able to prophecy thus to the child.

1 Samuel 2:1. And Hannah prayed, and said, My heart rejoiceth in the LORD, mine horn is exalted in the LORD: my mouth is enlarged over mine enemies; because I rejoice in thy salvation.
*10. The adversaries of the LORD shall be broken to pieces; out of heaven shall he thunder upon them: **the LORD shall judge the ends of the earth; and he shall give strength unto his king, and exalt the horn of his anointed**.*

Exalt the horn of his anointed.
In the realm of the spirit horns signify the power, authority and dominion of a king. In other words, Hannah was praying and prophesying that God would exalt the dominion and authority of Samuel. If Hannah referred to Samuel as king and Samuel was the son of her vows and Samuel belonged to God, we can therefore see the connection between Samuel and Lemuel. Lemuel was not a physical king but

rather a spiritual nomenclature used to refer to a particular group of people, which I call the kingly seeds. If we see Lemuel as a spiritual vocabulary used in reference to Samuel, it becomes easy to understand the connection. Hannah in the prophesy to Lemuel in Proverbs thirty one was using spiritual vocabulary to prophecy to Samuel and as we have seen she was used to prophesying to him in such a manner, using the vocabulary of the spirit. These words in Proverbs thirty one could be the same words Hannah used to teach Samuel the Nazarite law and way of life. I would say whoever wrote Proverbs thirty-one borrowed Hannah's words. Interestingly, this was not the first time her words have been borrowed and used. Note that king David used her exact words at some point in his songs and psalms. Considering the relationship between Samuel and David I would say David got these writings from Samuel's archive or perhaps Samuel used his mother's writings (or things he learnt from his mother) to mentor David on the ways and manner of kings.

If Samuel could keep the record of the acts of David in a book he wrote himself (1 Chronicles 29:29), then you should understand how that he was a good record keeper; hence keeping the writings of his mother would be a treasured endeavour to him. Now let's see how Hannah's words were borrowed by king David.

HANNAH'S WORDS.

1 Samuel 2:8. **He raiseth up the poor out of the dust, and lifteth up the beggar from the dunghill, to set them among princes, and to make them inherit the throne of glory:** *for* *the pillars of the earth are the LORD's, and he hath set the world upon them.*

DAVID'S WORDS.

Psalm 113:7. **He raiseth up the poor out of the dust, and lifteth the needy out of the dunghill;**
8. **That he may set him with princes, even with the princes of his people.**
9. He maketh the barren woman to keep house, and to be a joyful mother of children. Praise ye the LORD.

He maketh the barren woman to keep house, and to be a joyful mother of children. This statement is clearly in reference to Hannah. We can see therefore that somehow David and Solomon learnt some things from Hannah. They found her writings archived with Samuel useful and applied it to their own writings in songs, psalms and proverbs. So we can see how that the prophesy to Lemuel is from Hannah to Samuel.

Samuel was Hannah's Lemuel; he was her kingly seed. The words of Hannah to Lemuel because it was a prophecy (a statement made about the future and uttered under divine inspiration) apply to all the Lemuels or to all the kingly seeds. Going by the meaning of Lemuel (belonging to God) we can easily attribute this to the kingly seeds because as firstborns they belong to God and must be dedicated to God.
Now that established, that Lemuel refers to the kingly seeds. We can now see how the word to Lemuel by his mother applies to all kingly seeds.

Hannah in her prophecy revealed that there are two things that destroy the kingly seeds. They include women and alcohol. We know how the woman Delilah destroyed the kingly seed Samson and cut short his destiny on the earth. And she went on to prophecy how alcohol destroys kingly seeds as seen in Proverbs thirty-one. Besides the prophesy of Hannah we see that other prophets have also prophesied about the woes that accompany those who are given to alcohol.

Isaiah 5:11. **Woe unto them that rise up early in the morning, that they may follow strong drink;** *that continue until night, till wine inflame them!*
22. **Woe unto them that are mighty to drink wine,** *and men of strength to mingle strong drink:*

Proverbs 23:29. **Who hath woe? who hath sorrow?** *who hath contentions? who hath babbling? who hath wounds without cause? who hath redness of eyes?*
30. **They that tarry long at the wine; they that go to seek mixed wine.**
31. Look not thou upon the wine when it is red, when it giveth his colour in the cup, when it moveth itself aright.
32. **At the last it biteth like a serpent, and stingeth like an adder.**
33. Thine eyes shall behold strange women, and thine heart shall utter perverse things.
34. Yea, thou shalt be as he that lieth down in the midst of the sea, or as he that lieth upon the top of a mast.
35. They have stricken me, shalt thou say, and I was not sick; they have beaten me, and I felt it not: when shall I awake? I will seek it yet again.

Alcohol will pervert the judgment of the kingly seeds, it would not only affect a part of them but it would take control of their entire being: spirit, soul and body. The kingly seeds are meant to be filled with the Holy Spirit and not alcohol because alcohol and the Holy Spirit do not mix at all. When John the Baptist was to be born, it was said of him that he would be filled with the Holy Spirit and as a result of that no alcohol should come in contact with him, either from his mother directly (Luke 1:15).

This knowledge of alcohol and the kingly seeds is very important because what we eat or let into our belly affects our ability to make the right decisions. Speaking about Jesus in prophecy, it was said that butter and honey shall he eat in other to be able to reject evil and choose good (Isaiah 7:14-15). We see therefore that our ability to make the right choices in life depends on what we let into our belly. Letting alcohol into our belly will pervert our choices and ultimately hinder our fulfilment of purpose.

Isaiah 7:14. Therefore the Lord himself shall give you a sign; Behold, a virgin shall conceive, and bear a son, and shall call his name Immanuel.
*15. **Butter and honey shall he eat, that he may know to refuse the evil, and choose the good.***

The kingly seed, John the Baptist ate locust and wild honey, which made him fierce against evil (Mark 1:6). We see therefore that alcohol will hinder the fulfilment of the purpose of the kingly seeds. Alcohol will destroy the kingly seeds. Don't be enticed by its redness. It can sting like an adder. The devil uses it to sting and destroy the kingly seeds. If you must preserve your life, destiny and calling as a kingly seed, you must stay away from alcohol.

In closing this section, I would like to state this common observation. You know many women after giving birth, in a bid to have breast milk for the child; they are asked to drink alcohol, palm wine or other kinds of wine. What is however, unknown to these women is the fact that by doing this, the first food the baby takes in after birth is alcohol and this could have a lot of influence on the child. Who knows if this is the reason why we have many wine bibbers in such areas where this is practiced. As we have seen from scriptures, this is not allowed for the mothers of the kingly seeds.

Chapter 6

ABRAHAM AND SARAH

ISAAC

Genesis 17:1. And when Abram was ninety years old and nine, the LORD appeared to Abram, and said unto him, I am the Almighty God; walk before me, and be thou perfect.

2. And I will make my covenant between me and thee, and will multiply thee exceedingly.

4. As for me, behold, my covenant is with thee, and thou shalt be a father of many nations.

5. Neither shall thy name any more be called Abram, but thy name shall be Abraham; for a father of many nations have I made thee.

6. And I will make thee exceeding fruitful, and I will make nations of thee, and kings shall come out of thee.

10. This is my covenant, which ye shall keep, between me and you and thy seed after thee; Every man child among you shall be circumcised.

11. And ye shall circumcise the flesh of your foreskin; and it shall be a token of the covenant betwixt me and you.

15. And God said unto Abraham, As for Sarai thy wife, thou shalt not call her name Sarai, but Sarah shall her name be.
16. And I will bless her, and give thee a son also of her: yea, I will bless her, and she shall be a mother of nations; kings of people shall be of her.
17. Then Abraham fell upon his face, and laughed, and said in his heart, Shall a child be born unto him that is an hundred years old? and shall Sarah, that is ninety years old, bear?
19. And God said, Sarah thy wife shall bear thee a son indeed; and thou shalt call his name Isaac: and I will establish my covenant with him for an everlasting covenant, and with his seed after him.
21. But my covenant will I establish with Isaac, which Sarah shall bear unto thee at this set time in the next year.
24. And Abraham was ninety years old and nine, when he was circumcised in the flesh of his foreskin.

In this chapter we look at the couple Abraham and Sarah, the kingly seed from this union is Isaac. Abraham and Sarah were the first couple with the call of barrenness. They hold the template or perfect example for everyone with this call. We therefore look unto Abraham and Sarah as a perfect example of those with the call of barrenness. Everyone with this call must learn from them. The LORD speaking in the book of Isaiah chapter fifty one verse one and two concerning our calling, encouraged us to look unto Abraham and Sarah as the rocks from where we were cut out. In other words God was encouraging us to learn from Abraham and Sarah about the call of barrenness. God made us to understand that He called Abraham, blessed him, turned his wilderness into Eden, and turned his desert into a garden. That is, turned their barrenness into fruitfulness.

Isaiah 51:1. Hearken to me, ye that follow after righteousness, ye that seek the LORD: look unto the rock whence ye are hewn, and to the hole of the pit whence ye are digged.
2. Look unto Abraham your father, and unto Sarah that bare you: for I called him alone, and blessed him, and increased him.
3. For the LORD shall comfort Zion: he will comfort all her waste places; and he will make her wilderness like Eden, and her desert like the garden of the LORD; joy and gladness shall be found therein, thanksgiving, and the voice of melody.

God wants us to learn from this scripture that just as He turned the barrenness of Abraham and Sarah into fruitfulness, He will also do same for everyone with this call. The men with this call must understand with their wives. It's not like Abraham was not fertile, it was the wife that was infertile but he had to understand with his wife, he did not despise her. He understood that the power to conceive was not in her hand but in God's hands.

Parents with this call do not die early, they live long to enjoy the fruit of their labour. You know many people get anxious about bearing children late in life, thinking they will not enjoy their children. ***Those with this call do not need to be anxious about having children late in life because God will satisfy them with long life to enjoy the fruit of their labour.*** Long life for this people is actually a part of God's compensation plan for shutting their womb to bring forth late in life and for having this call upon their life. We see this truth in the life of those in the bible who had this call eg. Abraham, Isaac, Jacob, Zechariah etc. and their wives. Therefore those with this call do not need to be anxious about being late in childbirth.

From scriptures we see that, even though Abraham had Isaac at 100 years, he lived long enough to see his covenant son Isaac get married. Samson's father and mother witnessed Samson's marriage as well. Isaac lived to see his children's children. Jacob also lived to see his children's children. All these are men who had the call of barrenness upon their life.

Patience is an important virtue for those with this call. They must be patient to wait for the appointed time of life. From scriptures we see that Abraham was patient with God but Sarah was not. We see that, God appeared to Abraham first at 75 years and gave him the first promise (Genesis 12:1-4). Abraham left the land of Haran at 75 years and the promised seed was fulfilled when he was 100 years (That is 25 years after the promise). Interestingly, ten years after the promise was given (when Abraham was 85 years) discouragement set in, Sarah got tired of waiting and compelled Abraham to marry her maid Hagar. Unfortunately, the promise still would not be fulfilled for another 15 years and Sarah had to spend the next fifteen years after her suggestion, under the emotional torture of Hagar. If she had waited on God she could have had less stress while waiting for the fulfilment of the promise. (Genesis 16:2-4).

When we wait patiently for God to fulfil His promise we enjoy peace, according to prophet Isaiah in Isaiah 26:3, He said *"God will keep us in perfect peace, when we trust and wait for Him"*.

It's important to note that, every act of obedience to God brings you closer to the fulfilment of the promise. And the destiny of the children is tied to the obedience of their fathers. We see that at age 99 God appeared again to Abraham with a final command before the fulfilment of the promise. God asked Abraham to circumcise himself and without delay Abraham got circumcised at the age of 99 thus bringing himself into an eternal covenant with God. Abraham didn't understand the essence of his circumcision but his obedience to God's instruction prepared him for the fulfilment of the promise (Genesis 17:10-27).

I believe all the men whose wives have the call of barrenness in our time today have the same calling with Abraham, and like Abraham was obedient to God and received the promise they are also expected to be obedient to the commands of God to receive the promise. Also like Abraham's faithfulness was tested, their faithfulness will also be tested.

We must understand that, the promises of God do not often come on a platter of gold. The conviction of our calling and absolute trust in God will often be tested. Many with this call will be tempted to look for alternative measures of being fruitful outside of God. I strongly believe that the suggestion of Sarah for Abraham to lay with Hagar was a test, which Abraham failed. Perhaps if Abraham had overcome that temptation, Isaac could have arrived earlier.

This test could continue even after the promised kingly seed has been born. Abraham was tried to sacrifice his only son, the promised kingly seed to God. From this encounter I see that God wants parents with the calling of barrenness to be willing to surrender their children to Him. God will test your willingness to submit your long awaited precious child to Him. We must understand that every firstborn child belongs to God, we do not have the capacity to take care of such children, only God does. We must therefore hand them over to God for His care and use. This I believe was the mystery that happened with Isaac on the altar, we also see it in Samson and Samuel. These children must be sacrificed or surrendered to God in other to fulfil their purpose on the earth. Until we surrender these children to God for his use, God would not take over their affairs. Abraham passed the test of giving Isaac on the altar as a living sacrifice for God's glory and use. You will be required to do same.

THINGS TO LEARN FROM ABRAHAM AND SARAH

ABRAHAM

1. Abraham was charitable and generous.

He was charitable to all including strangers. He took Lot his nephew with him, trained him until he became a man of his own. He had living with him over three hundred male servants (beside women) who were born in his house. His house was more like a community. All these people were under his care.

Abraham was so generous that when he finds you as much as close to his house, he will persuade you to eat or take a drink in his house. He entertained strangers until he entertained angels and God. Thank God for Sarah who also had the same spirit of hospitality because she eventually became the one running around to get the food ready.

Genesis 18:1. And the LORD appeared unto him in the plains of Mamre: and he sat in the tent door in the heat of the day;
2. And he lift up his eyes and looked, and, lo, three men stood by him: and when he saw them, he ran to meet them from the tent door, and bowed himself toward the ground,
3. And said, My Lord, if now I have found favour in thy sight, pass not away, I pray thee, from thy servant:
4. Let a little water, I pray you, be fetched, and wash your feet, and rest yourselves under the tree:
5. And I will fetch a morsel of bread, and comfort ye your hearts; after that ye shall pass on: for therefore are ye come to your servant. And they said, So do, as thou hast said.
6. And Abraham hastened into the tent unto Sarah, and said, Make ready quickly three measures of fine meal, knead it, and make cakes upon the hearth.
7. And Abraham ran unto the herd, and fetcht a calf tender and good, and gave it unto a young man; and he hasted to dress it.
*8. And he took butter, and milk, and the calf which he had dressed, and set it before them; and **he stood by them under the tree, and they did eat.***
9. And they said unto him, Where is Sarah thy wife? And he said, Behold, in the tent.
10. And he said, I will certainly return unto thee according to

the time of life; and, lo, Sarah thy wife shall have a son. And Sarah heard it in the tent door, which was behind him.

I keep wondering how long it took to get the food ready and what Abraham could have been discussing during this time with the Trinity who came visiting. Only friends can have a meaningful discussion for hours without getting bored. Abraham built friendship with God through hospitality. Abraham was not called a friend of God because he believed or obeyed God but he became a friend of God on the platform of hospitality.

In ending this point about hospitality, I would like you to take note of this. Note that Abraham served his guests by himself, he did not send his servants (though he had as many as over three hundred servants). And note the striking thing he did, **"And *he stood by them under the tree, and they did eat.*** Note that he did not sit, he stood like a servant. Abraham humbled himself before his guests. Perhaps he was standing close by to know if they need anything in other to attend to it immediately. And that was when God spoke life to Sarah's womb and opened it for the conception of Isaac.

2. Abraham was an intercessor.

He interceded for the salvation of many whom he didn't even know. God does not hide His plans from those with this calling because he expects them to be intercessors for the lost. By virtue of their calling, they are intercessors by design; as such God expects them to stand in the gap for others. God expects them to be selfless.

Genesis 18:16. And the men rose up from thence, and looked toward Sodom: and Abraham went with them to bring them on the way.

17. And the LORD said, Shall I hide from Abraham that thing which I do;

19. For I know him, that he will command his children and his household after him, and they shall keep the way of the LORD, to do justice and judgment; that the LORD may bring upon Abraham that which he hath spoken of him.

20. And the LORD said, Because the cry of Sodom and Gomorrah is great, and because their sin is very grievous;

21. I will go down now, and see whether they have done altogether according to the cry of it, which is come unto me; and if not, I will know.

22. And the men turned their faces from thence, and went toward Sodom: but Abraham stood yet before the LORD.

23. And Abraham drew near, and said, Wilt thou also destroy the righteous with the wicked?

24. Peradventure there be fifty righteous within the city: wilt thou also destroy and not spare the place for the fifty righteous that are therein?

25. That be far from thee to do after this manner, to slay the righteous with the wicked: and that the righteous should be as the wicked, that be far from thee: Shall not the Judge of all the earth do right?

26. And the LORD said, If I find in Sodom fifty righteous within the city, then I will spare all the place for their sakes.

32. And he said, Oh let not the Lord be angry, and I will speak yet but this once: Peradventure ten shall be found there. And he said, I will not destroy it for ten's sake.

33. And the LORD went his way, as soon as he had left

communing with Abraham: and Abraham returned unto his place.

Abraham became a mediator between God and man, seeking the salvation of men from the judgement, wrath and anger of God.

3. Abraham believed God. He was a man of faith.

Romans 4:3. For what saith the scripture? Abraham believed God, and it was counted unto him for righteousness.
18. Who against hope believed in hope, that he might become the father of many nations; according to that which was spoken, So shall thy seed be.
19. And being not weak in faith, he considered not his own body now dead, when he was about an hundred years old, neither yet the deadness of Sara's womb:
20. He staggered not at the promise of God through unbelief; but was strong in faith, giving glory to God;
21. And being fully persuaded that, what he had promised, he was able also to perform.
22. And therefore it was imputed to him for righteousness.

Abraham was not impotent when he received the promise of fruitfulness from God, otherwise how could he have had Ishmael through Hagar. However, God allowed him to get to a point of impotence (which results from old age) to prove that no matter how bad or worse a matter is, He God can still turn it around. At this point Abraham began to hope against hope. At first it was only his wife Sarah who was infertile, at this time it was a single problem. And later on Abraham became impotent due to old age, at this time it became double problem, which made the problem worse. Ordinarily, one should feel discouraged that if the problem could not be solved when it was one, how much more when the problem doubles. Nevertheless, Abraham when faced with this double problem hoped even more. He hoped against hope. He moved from hoping, to believing in the same hope.

4. He was promptly obedient to God's instructions

Abraham was obedient to God's commandments and instructions. His prompt obedience secured a trans-generational blessing for his children.

Genesis 26:4. And I will make thy seed to multiply as the stars of heaven, and will give unto thy seed all these countries; and in thy seed shall all the nations of the earth be blessed;
5. Because that Abraham obeyed my voice, and kept my charge, my commandments, my statutes, and my laws.

Obedience is a fundamental requirement; if we must see the blessings and promises of God come to pass in our life. For those with this calling, we are admonished to be obedient to God's instructions, commands, statutes and laws as Abraham was.

5. Abraham was hopeful and expectant.

Abraham was not just a man of faith but he was also a faithful man. Very importantly Abraham was hopeful and expectant that God will fulfil His promise to him.

When hope failed Abraham, he chose to believe in the same hope that had failed him. Abraham stopped hoping and started believing in hope. He moved from hoping on hope to believing in hope. To him hope was very tangible. To hope is to be expectant. Abraham was still expectant even when it seemed like all hope was lost. He kept believing that his expectations will be delivered to him according to God's word. He kept expecting God to fulfil his promise to him. For you with this calling, you must be expectant of your God ordained kingly child and God will bring it to pass. Our expectations act like a magnetic force or cord that pulls our blessings from the spiritual realm into the natural realm. No wonder as long as our expectations are connected to our desired blessings, it doesn't get cut off. (Proverbs 23:18)

SARAH

1. Sarah believed and trusted in God

Sarah was full of faith in God. Though God did not speak to her directly, but the fact that she heard what God said about her through her husband Abraham, she believed God.

Hebrews 11:11. Through faith also Sara herself received strength to conceive seed, and was delivered of a child when she was past age, because she judged him faithful who had promised.

We are not only expected to believe God only when we hear directly from Him. When we believe God even when we didn't hear His message to us directly from Him, is a reflection of faith. We also see that Sarah believed God even when the situation seemed impossible. She knew that she had passed the age of child bearing yet she believed God to bring His promise to pass. Perhaps you have passed the age of child bearing, but this is the time to believe God even more. Its natural to put to birth before menopause but it becomes supernatural to put to birth when you have passed menopause. For those with this call, the child you are expecting is a supernatural child not a natural child, therefore expect the child to be brought forth according to its nature; supernaturally.

2. Sarah was humble and submissive to her husband

Sarah was very submissive to Abraham her husband to a point that she called him her lord. She saw Abraham as her lord and king and submitted to him as her lord.

*1 Peter 3:1. Likewise, ye wives, be in subjection to your own husbands; that, if any obey not the word, **they also may without the word be won by the conversation of the wives;***
*4. But let it be the hidden man of the heart, in that which is not corruptible, even the **ornament of a meek and quiet spirit, which is in the sight of God of great price.***
5. For after this manner in the old time the holy women also, who trusted in God, adorned themselves, being in subjection unto their own husbands:
6. Even as Sara obeyed Abraham, calling him lord: whose daughters ye are, as long as ye do well, and are not afraid with any amazement.

From the above scripture we see that submission is a powerful tool for the conversion and salvation of husbands. Wives can through submission win their husbands heart, love, attention, cooperation, respect and even soul. Sarah was submissive to her husband and all women are admonished to be thus submissive.

3. Sarah was obedient to her husband

Sarah was very obedient to her husband Abraham, as we have seen in first Peter three verse six. She obeyed her husband without asking any questions. Even at old age she was still the one cooking for her household. Sarah at age eighty-nine was still cooking for Abraham and doing his bidding, until she obeyed him and cooked for God the Trinity. What? God the Trinity? You may ask. Yes! God the Trinity. Yes, Sarah cooked for God. God the Father, the Son and the Holy Spirit came in the form of three men and visited Abraham in his house.

*Genesis 18:1. And **the LORD appeared unto him** in the plains of Mamre: and he sat in the tent door in the heat of the day;*
*2. And he lift up his eyes and looked, and, lo, **three men stood by him**: and when he saw them, he ran to meet them from the tent door, and bowed himself toward the ground,*
*3. And said, **My Lord**, if now I have found favour in thy sight, pass not away, I pray thee, from thy servant:*
4. Let a little water, I pray you, be fetched, and wash your feet, and rest yourselves under the tree:
5. And I will fetch a morsel of bread, and comfort ye your hearts; after that ye shall pass on: for therefore are ye come to your servant. And they said, So do, as thou hast said.

*6. And Abraham hastened into the tent unto **Sarah, and said, Make ready quickly three measures of fine meal, knead it, and make cakes upon the hearth.***

The three men in the above scripture were the Godhead in human form, note it did not say angels; it said the LORD appeared unto him. This was the encounter which was spoken of by the Lord Jesus in John gospel chapter eight verse fifty-six that **"Abraham rejoiced to see my day: he saw it and was glad".** This encounter between the Lord Jesus and Abraham was what brought gladness, joy and laughter to Abraham and his family.

Note that it was the Lord Jesus that Abraham was speaking with all through the time he was with the Trinity. How do I know? Note the capitalisation of the word **Lord**. The capitalisation of only the letter **"L"** as in "**Lord**" is often used to refer to Jesus (Romans 16:24), the word "**LORD**" (all capitalised) refers to God the Father while the word lord (all in small letters) is used to represent a human lord (1 Peter 3:6). So we see Abraham communicating with the Trinity through the Lord Jesus. In truth we are meant to speak to God the Father through Jesus, if we understand this, it becomes clearer to us why we are asked to make our requests through the name of Jesus Christ (John 16:23-24).

That understood, let's move on to what happened when God ate Sarah's food. And when God ate her food, He was moved to speak to Sarah's womb immediately. And God said to Abraham, where is Sarah thy wife?

Genesis 18:9. And they said unto him, **Where is Sarah thy wife?** *And he said, Behold, in the tent.*
10. And he said, **I will certainly return unto thee according to the time of life; and, lo, Sarah thy wife shall have a son.** *And Sarah heard it in the tent door, which was behind him.*
11. Now Abraham and Sarah were old and well stricken in age; and it ceased to be with Sarah after the manner of women.

And that was how Sarah's womb was opened in her old age for the conception of Isaac. I tell you! There is something about hospitality that moves God to bring His promise to pass in our life. Remember what the Lord Jesus said, *"Verily, inasmuch as you have done good to the least of my brethren, you have done it unto me"*. Your hospitality to anyone can move God to bring His promises speedily to pass in your life.

Note that Abraham and Sarah had many servants and maids yet they chose to entertain the strangers themselves. When Abraham suddenly and urgently asked Sarah to cook she hastily obeyed without any question or hesitation. Perhaps other women could have said, *"Abraham, you are giving too much attention to strangers, did they tell you they were hungry?"* Perhaps other women could have said, *"Abraham, you are giving more attention to strangers than you are giving to me"*.

Like Sarah every woman with this call are admonished to obey their husbands without asking questions. In obeying your husband who is the visioner, you can welcome and entertain God into your life and family.
Note that, for you with this calling, you will likely be visited

by God to herald the arrival of your precious seed. Therefore be expectant and be obedient to your husband because your obedience to your husband could help you not to miss God's timing when He comes knocking. Note that God did not appear to the woman but to the man, which tells us that God will always reveal himself to the man and the cooperation of the woman is required for God to move freely in their midst. Imagine if Sarah had started making faces or started quarrelling her husband when God visited. God would have left the home if He were not welcomed. Also note that God did not come for Abraham, He came for Sarah. Sarah was the one who was blessed and whose womb was opened after the meal, even though the Trinity came through Abraham to enter the home.

4. She was cooperative with her husband

The cooperation of the wife is very important for the fulfilment of their purpose. Interestingly, the call of barrenness is not a calling that one person can fulfil; this is a calling that requires two people to fulfil. Therefore the cooperation of the wife is highly required for the fulfilment of this calling. Sarah cooperated with her husband, and did everything he told her even when it was not convenient.

Genesis 12:11. And it came to pass, when he was come near to enter into Egypt, that he said unto Sarai his wife, Behold now, I know that thou art a fair woman to look upon:
12. Therefore it shall come to pass, when the Egyptians shall see thee, that they shall say, This is his wife: and they will kill me, but they will save thee alive.

13. Say, I pray thee, thou art my sister: that it may be well with me for thy sake; and my soul shall live because of thee.

Sarah worked together with her husband to see God's promise come to pass in their life. Every woman with this calling is expected to cooperate with their husbands who happen to be the bearers of the vision.

ISAAC

Isaac was the first child that was conceived and born as a result of the call of barrenness. One very important thing we must learn from the life of Isaac is that Isaac was offered to God as a living sacrifice and as such all who are born as a result of this call must be offered unto God as a living sacrifice.

Hebrews 11:17. By faith Abraham, when he was tried, offered up Isaac: and he that had received the promises offered up his only begotten son,

Abraham offered up Isaac his only begotten son...

Note that even though Isaac was not offered unto God naturally but spiritually in Abraham's heart, Abraham had already offered up Isaac to God as a living sacrifice. In other words we may not offer our called children naturally by killing them but we must offer them up spiritually unto God.

THE ESSENCE OF THE SACRIFICE OF ISAAC

The hallmark of Isaac's life was that Isaac was a living sacrifice unto God. By becoming a living sacrifice, he became dead to the flesh and alive in the spirit. The hallmark of the life of every child begotten of this calling is to be a living sacrifice unto God. We see from scriptures that all the children born from this calling were surrendered to God as a living sacrifice. We see that Samson and John the Baptist were separated as Nazarites unto God right from the womb. We also see that the moment Hannah made up her mind to give up the child God gives to her as a living sacrifice, God answered her immediately and gave her Samuel.

1 Samuel 1:11. And she vowed a vow, and said, O LORD of hosts, if thou wilt indeed look on the affliction of thine handmaid, and remember me, and not forget thine handmaid, but wilt give unto thine handmaid a man child, then I will give him unto the LORD all the days of his life, and there shall no rasor come upon his head.

It's important to understand that God wants every parent with this calling, to surrender or offer unto Him their firstborn children as a living sacrifice just as Abraham offered Isaac as a living sacrifice unto God. Not surrendering the child in your heart as a living sacrifice to God could cause the arrival of the seed to linger much longer until you finally make up your mind to surrender the child to God. I realise by divine inspiration that when God wants to ordain an important mystery for the first time He does it in a dramatic way, to reveal its essence and to serve as a template for us to understand what happens when it occurs again in the future. For instance, look at the mystery of water baptism, the resurrection, Holy Ghost baptism etc. When the church was being baptised in the Holy Ghost for the first time it was very dramatic, with rushing winds and cloven tongues of fire on the head of those who were being baptised, giving them the appearance of a candle. After that Pentecost experience, today when we get baptised in the Holy Ghost none of these dramatic scenes are seen, however we cannot miss the essence of being set on fire for God, as our spirit, which is the candle of the Lord, is set on fire.

The story of the sacrifice of Isaac is not just a story about the test of the willingness of Abraham to sacrifice Isaac but a picture of what must happen to all the firstborn seed from the barren wombs. This is what I call *the ordinance of absolute surrender to God* or *the ordinance of the living sacrifice*.

Even though Isaac was not sacrificed physically, he was sacrificed spiritually; the lamb that was revealed to Abraham and was used for the sacrifice was a spiritual representation of Isaac. More like what happens when we see Jesus as the Lamb of God.

The kingly seeds are called to live a sacrificial and selfless lifestyle and as such must sacrifice their will, ego, appetite and desires to God because it is only when this is done that they can be used by God to fulfil their purpose, hence this sacrifice is very important even before the child is born. Interestingly, this sacrifice is fulfilled in the heart of the parents as revealed in the case of Hannah, Manoah and Elizabeth.

THE LIFESTYLE OF ISAAC

There are many good qualities in the life of Isaac however there are two important qualities in his life that we must take note of.

1. ISAAC WAS A PEACEFUL MAN

We see that when Isaac was asked to live the land of Gerar by the king, he left without hesitation; he did not think that because he was greater than the kingdom, he should fight and conquer the kingdom for himself. We also see that even when his men dug a well and the philistines stopped them, he did not resist them, he only moved to another location and dug another well, until the philistines got tired of striving with him.

Genesis 26:18. And Isaac digged again the wells of water, which they had digged in the days of Abraham his father; for the philistines had stopped them after the death of Abraham: and he called their names after the names by which his father had called them.
19. And Isaac's servants digged in the valley, and found there a well of springing water.
20. And the herdmen of Gerar did strive with Isaac's herdmen, saying, The water is ours: and he called the name of the well Esek; because they strove with him.
21. And they digged another well, and strove for that also:and he called the name of it Sitnah.

2. ISAAC WAS PERSISTENT AND CONSISTENT

Isaac was persistent and consistent in the pursuit of his vision. He had a vision to continue the vision and legacy of his father Abraham. Part of the vision was to continue and sustain the call of barrenness through marriage, which was why he was grieved when his son Esau married a Hittite (Genesis 26:34-35). Also part of his vision to continue the legacy of his father was to continue to dig the wells of water that his father had started, calling them by the same name that his father had called them. The digging of wells at that time was a huge business venture for the Abraham's family. In truth, this venture was the secret to Abraham's wealth and abundance. The fruitfulness of any land and nation depends on water; now imagine a family having control over springs of water (that is; the purest kind of water), especially in the time of famine. That should give you an idea of the importance of this business venture to the Abraham's family. Isaac sought to sustain this family business and was persistent and consistent in its pursuit. He kept digging these wells despite the resistance from the philistines until he finally had his way. When he digs a well, the philistines will claim that it belongs to them, he will peacefully leave it for them and dig another well somewhere else, until finally through his consistency God made room for them and the philistines stopped striving with them.

Note that digging wells and finding water at that time was not an easy task, it was something that required the help of God. Until your eyes were opened by God to see where water is, you will be wasting your efforts. Until God opened Hagar's eyes she could not see the wells of water in the wilderness of Beer-Sheba.

Genesis 21:19. And God opened her eyes, and she saw a well of water; and she went, and filled the bottle with water, and gave the lad drink.

Abraham's eyes were opened by God to know where to dig to find water, such that he had control over water at that time. The philistines could not dig and find water on their own, as God did not help them. In those days you had to pray to God for your eyes to be opened to see the wells of water and the philistines did not know God neither did they pray to him. And not being able to see and dig their own wells they had to strive with both Abraham and Isaac to take their wells of water because on their own they did not know where to dig to find water.

Isaac through persistence and consistency sustained the Abraham's family heritage and well water business venture.

Genesis 26:22. And he removed from thence, and digged another well; and for that they strove not: and he called the name of it Rehoboth; and he said, For now the LORD hath made room for us, and we shall be fruitful in the land.
23. And he went up from thence to Beer-sheba.
24. And the LORD appeared unto him the same night, and said, I am the God of Abraham thy father: fear not, for I am with thee, and will bless thee, and multiply thy seed for my servant Abraham's sake.
*25. And **he builded an altar there**, and **called upon the name of the LORD** and pitched his tent there: and **there Isaac's servants digged a well.***

*32. And it came to pass the same day, that Isaac's servants came, and told him concerning the well which they had digged, and said unto him, **We have found water.***
33. And he called it Shebah: therefore the name of the city is Beer-sheba unto this day.

3. ISAAC WAS A MAN OF PRAYER

Isaac was a man of prayer. At every opportunity he had Isaac always raised up an altar unto the LORD. An altar often represents a place of prayer. Isaac understood the timing of God; he knew that whenever God appeared to him, it was time to raise up an altar of prayer. He knew that whenever God reveals himself, his word or his promises to him it was a time to pray for the fulfilment of that word of promise.

Isaac learnt how to raise an altar of prayer from his father Abraham and this he transferred to his children.

Genesis 12:7. And the LORD appeared unto Abram, and said, Unto thy seed will I give this land: and there builded he an altar unto the LORD, who appeared unto him.
8. And he removed from thence unto a mountain on the east of Bethel, and pitched his tent, having Bethel on the west, and Hai on the east: and there he builded an altar unto the LORD, and called upon the name of the LORD.

It takes men of prayer to fulfil the calling of barrenness. Interestingly those with this calling are given the grace to pray, because it is a component of their calling and assignment.

THE GREATNESS OF ISAAC

The greatness of Isaac was greater than that of an entire kingdom, such that the king of Gerar where Isaac dwelt had to ask Isaac to leave the land as he had become greater than them.

The greatness of Isaac depended on his obedience to God's instruction. Isaac obeyed the instruction of the LORD not to go to Egypt but to remain in the land of Gerar where his father was.

Genesis 26:2. And the LORD appeared unto him, and said, Go not down into Egypt; dwell in the land which I shall tell thee of:
3. Sojourn in this land, and I will be with thee, and will bless thee; for unto thee, and unto thy seed, I will give all these countries, and I will perform the oath which I sware unto Abraham thy father;
4. And I will make thy seed to multiply as the stars of heaven, and will give unto thy seed all these countries; and in thy seed shall all the nations of the earth be blessed;
5. Because that Abraham obeyed my voice, and kept my charge, my commandments, my statutes, and my laws.

God's promise to Abraham and to his seeds and to all who have the same calling was territorially dependent. Such that, understanding the territory, which we have been given dominion per time, will help us fulfil our calling with ease. Jacob had a territorial dominion over the nation of Israel. Joseph was given the territorial dominion over Egypt. Isaac at this time only had territorial dominion over the land of

Gerar. His dominion was so great that the king of Gerar had to come to Isaac after his departure from the land of Gerar for a peace treaty and to enter into a covenant with Isaac that he should not hurt them in the future.

Genesis 26:12. Then Isaac sowed in that land, and received in the same year an hundredfold: and the LORD blessed him.
13. And the man waxed great, and went forward, and grew until he became very great:
14. For he had possession of flocks, and possessions of herds, and great store of servants: and the Philistines envied him.
16. And Abimelech said unto Isaac, Go from us; for thou art much mightier than we.
17. And Isaac departed thence, and pitched his tent in the valley of Gerar, and dwelt there.
26. Then Abimelech went to him from Gerar, and Ahuzzath one of his friends, and Phichol the chief captain of his army.
28. And they said, We saw certainly that the LORD was with thee: and we said, Let there be now an oath betwixt us, even betwixt us and thee, and let us make a covenant with thee;
29. That thou wilt do us no hurt, as we have not touched thee, and as we have done unto thee nothing but good, and have sent thee away in peace: thou art now the blessed of the LORD.

Chapter 7

ISAAC AND REBECCA

JACOB

Isaac and Rebecca were the second couple to fulfil the call of barrenness. Rebecca was Isaac's second cousin, that is, she was his father's brother's granddaughter. Isaac got married to Rebecca at age forty and had his twin children at age sixty, that is twenty years after marriage. This means that Rebecca was barren for twenty years after her marriage to Isaac.

Abraham died at one hundred and seventy five years, Isaac died at one hundred and eighty years. Though Abraham had his first child at old age, yet he saw his children and grandchildren.

*Genesis 25:20. And **Isaac was forty years old when he took Rebekah to wife**, the daughter of Bethuel the Syrian of Padan-aram, the sister to Laban the Syrian.*

21. And Isaac intreated the LORD for his wife, because she was barren: and the LORD was intreated of him, and Rebekah his wife conceived.

22. *And the children struggled together within her; and she said, If it be so, why am I thus? And she went to inquire of the LORD.*

23. *And the LORD said unto her, Two nations are in thy womb, and two manner of people shall be separated from thy bowels; and the one people shall be stronger than the other people; and the elder shall serve the younger.*

24. *And when her days to be delivered were fulfilled, behold, there were twins in her womb.*

25. *And the first came out red, all over like an hairy garment; and they called his name Esau.*

26. *And after that came his brother out, and his hand took hold on Esau's heel; and his name was called Jacob: and **Isaac was threescore years old when she bare them.***

27. *And the boys grew: and Esau was a cunning hunter, a man of the field; and Jacob was a plain man, dwelling in tents.*

*Genesis 35:28. And **the days of Isaac were an hundred and fourscore years.***

Much has been said about Isaac in the previous chapter, in this chapter the spotlight will be on Rebecca.

REBECCA

Rebecca was a beautiful woman who also had a beautiful heart. She was very respectful, hospitable and kind, even to strangers. She was kind enough to give Abraham's servant (a stranger she just met) water to drink as well as his camels.

And when the man asked if he could find a place in her fathers house to lodge, with excitement she told him that there is enough room and food for both him and his animals. That is how hospitable Rebecca was.

The marriage of Isaac and Rebecca was divinely orchestrated, God supernaturally brought Rebecca to be Isaac's wife. God was the matchmaker in their marriage. Without doubt we can see that they were brought together by God to fulfil the call of barrenness. For one to think that God would choose a barren woman to be the wife of his faithful and loved servant without a reason or purpose will be highly misplaced. God in His infinite wisdom could not have chosen a barren woman for his servant without a purpose. Isaac and Rebecca were brought together by God to fulfil the purpose of the call of barrenness.

You know many people say God is no more matchmaking couples in marriage. Well, that is not true at all. God is still in the business of matching or pairing couples for marriage, especially for the fulfilment of the call of barrenness. The wise king Solomon in his wisdom said, *"a prudent wife comes from God"* (Proverbs 19:14), meaning such women are rare to find and must be brought to a man by God. This kind of wife cannot be found by any man's effort, only God can find them and bring them to the man. Such was the case of Isaac and Rebecca. Rebecca was such a prudent woman. Her prudence can be seen in her orchestration of the blessing of Jacob by Isaac. Firstly, She knew and understood the prophesy about Jacob and knew that Jacob was the one who had the mantle of continuing the call of barrenness. She knew Jacob was the one called by God to fulfil the call of barrenness (Romans 9:10-12) and she worked prudently to ensure the fulfilment of the call (Genesis 27:43-46, Genesis 28:1-2). Secondly, she knew that by Esau's marriage to a Hittite he was completely out of the picture for the fulfilment of the call of barrenness and hence should not be the one to receive the blessing of the firstborn, since the call is tied to the firstborn. According to prophesy the blessing of the firstborn was to be proclaimed on Jacob, Isaac however could have proclaimed it on Esau if Rebecca had not intervened.

Genesis 25:22. And the children struggled together within her; and she said, If it be so, why am I thus? And she went to inquire of the LORD.
23. And the LORD said unto her, Two nations are in thy womb, and two manner of people shall be separated from thy bowels; and the one people shall be stronger than the other people; and the elder shall serve the younger.

Note that the prophesy was given to Rebecca directly by God, so Isaac may not be privy to it. It was only necessary for her to ensure the fulfilment of the prophesy and this she achieved with prudence. She didn't need to quarrel, fight or argue with her husband to achieve it but with prudence she had her way. Unlike other women who may want to enforce their right, she could have confronted her husband and said, NO, God told me that Jacob would be greater than Esau and should be the one to have the firstborn blessing but NO, she couldn't do that because she was too prudent to approach a matter like that. Like Rebecca, every woman with this calling is expected to deal prudently.

Rebecca was also a very faithful and dedicated woman, who would give anything for the fulfilment of a just cause. I believe God knew He could trust her to pursue the fulfilment of the call of barrenness and that was why He entrusted her with the prophesy of her children even before they were born. Even though in fulfilling this just cause it would require Rebecca to become an enemy of one of her sons, yet she ensured that the prophecy and call of barrenness was sustained despite the odds. If it were not for her the call of barrenness could have been interrupted at this point. This points to the reason why God is still the matchmaker in any marriage that is required for the fulfilment the call of barrenness.

Rebecca was highly instrumental in the fulfilment of Jacob's destiny. Without her help Jacob would not be properly guided and empowered for the fulfilment of his glorious destiny.

In summary we can see that Rebecca was...
   1. *Hospitable and kind.*
   2. *Humble and respectful.*
   3. *Highly Prudent.*
   4. *Faithful and dedicated.*
   5. *Divinely ordained to marry Isaac.*

JACOB

Jacob was the second kingly seed to be born out of the call of barrenness. He was born along with his brother Esau. Esau came out first; however, Jacob held unto Esau's heel and came out alongside with him. The nature of his birth earned him his name Jacob, which means *"holder of the heel"* or *"supplanter"*. Interestingly he lived according to his birth name until God had to change his name from Jacob to Israel. The life of Jacob is a clear picture that men with this calling are not immune to natural weaknesses. Wearing the human flesh comes with its own weaknesses, which also imparts on those with this calling. This truth is validated in the life of Samson. We also see that though those with this calling have a great destiny, yet their destiny can be affected by their given names and for them to fulfil their God ordained destiny, they must have a change of name to reflect what they are destined to be. God had to change Jacob's name before he could be ushered into his God ordained destiny. To validate this truth we see the name of his own grandfather changed from Abram to Abraham. We also see that God had to send an angel with the name John to Zechariah for John the Baptist to be so named. Perhaps to avoid having to change John's name at a later time in his life. We see that John was destined to live a short life, and as such he didn't have the luxury of time to learn from life's challenges and from his mistakes, so he had to be named purposefully at his birth.

Jacob was a very cunning and wise man from the womb. Right in the womb he hatched a plan to take his brother's birthright, however, he could not achieve this plan in the womb, perhaps because nature was stronger than him at that time. Yet he never gave up on his plan to overthrow his brother, he kept nurturing the plan after they were born and for many years he kept planning the takeover of his brother's birthright until he finally succeeded. Jacob was a master schemer from the womb, no wonder Esau didn't see it coming when he was being defrauded of his birthright. He was a man who wanted to defy nature from birth. His ability to cause animals to bring forth according to his desire by just looking at a rod is beyond human nature. Seeing the gate of heaven is beyond human nature. Wrestling with a heavenly being and overcoming him is beyond human nature. He was a man who defied human nature to fulfil his purpose. Many great feats he achieved were supernaturally empowered hence his ability to defy nature. For e.g. the conception of the unique breed of cattle were revealed to him in a dream by an angel of God.

Genesis 31:10. And it came to pass at the time that the cattle conceived, that I lifted up mine eyes, and saw in a dream, and, behold, the rams which leaped upon the cattle were ringstraked, speckled, and grisled.
11. And the angel of God spake unto me in a dream, saying, Jacob: And I said, Here am I.
12. And he said, Lift up now thine eyes, and see, all the rams which leap upon the cattle are ringstraked, speckled, and grisled: for I have seen all that Laban doeth unto thee.
13. I am the God of Bethel, where thou anointedst the pillar, and where thou vowedst a vow unto me: now arise, get thee out from this land, and return unto the land of thy kindred.

The mystery of the poplar rods was supernaturally revealed to him, which gave him an edge in his bargain with Laban.

Jacob was a wise and cunning man yet he was obedient to his parents. His obedience to his mother helped him to receive the blessing of the firstborn from his father.

Jacob married his first cousins, Leah and Rachel. Remember at this time consanguineal marriages were allowed, especially for the purpose of this calling. Leah and Rachel had the same calling of barrenness. They were both barren until God saw that she was not loved by Jacob and He opened her womb.

Rachel's womb was opened at God's will not at Jacob's request as we see in the case of Isaac who intreated God for his wife. Note that all through the time Rachel was barren, it was not recorded that Jacob prayed to God to open his wife's womb. It was until God remembered her that He opened her womb. I cannot say for sure but I believe it's possible that the prayer of a called husband could shorten the time of barrenness of his wife and hasten the fulfilment of the call.

THE CALL OF JACOB

Jacob was called by God to fulfil the call of barrenness. The call of Jacob to fulfil this call is revealed in the book of Isaiah.

Isaiah 48:12. Hearken unto me, **O Jacob and Israel, my called;** *I am he; I am the first, I also am the last.*
15. I, even I, have spoken; yea, **I have called him**: *I have brought him, and he shall make his way prosperous.*
18. O that thou hadst hearkened to my commandments! then had thy peace been as a river, and thy righteousness as the waves of the sea:
19. **Thy seed also had been as the sand,** *and the offspring of*

thy bowels like the gravel thereof; his name should not have been cut off nor destroyed from before me.

God speaking to Jacob and by extension the entire Israel said; if Jacob had harkened to His commandments (which I believe is the commandment that they should not marry from the prohibited tribes), Jacob's seed and offspring wouldn't have been cut off or destroyed. We have seen from previous chapters how the transgression of the children of Israel polluted the kingly seed. And here is God in his word through Isaiah to Israel speaking about how the disobedience of Israel to his commandments has affected Jacob's offspring.

This points to the truth that the calling of Jacob that God was referring to above was the call of barrenness.

THE GREATNESS OF JACOB

Jacob was very great in his time, of all who have had the call before him; he had the highest number of children, which today are referred to as the twelve tribes of Israel.

Jacob was a principality, a territorial commander over the nation of Israel. Through him the nation of Israel was born, he had spiritual control over the entire nation of Israel. As a person he had power with God and with men, and as a nation he was unconquerable. While in Egypt the children of Israel became mightier than the Egyptians such that it became a great concern to the Egyptians.

Exodus 1:7. And the children of Israel were fruitful, and increased abundantly, and multiplied, and waxed exceeding mighty; and the land was filled with them.
8. Now there arose up a new king over Egypt, which knew not Joseph.
9. And he said unto his people, Behold, the people of the children of Israel are more and mightier than we:

Jacob enjoyed the help of God, which made him greater than the nation of Egypt at the time and even stronger than their enemies.

Psalm 105:23. Israel also came into Egypt; and Jacob sojourned in the land of Ham.
24. And he increased his people greatly; and made them stronger than their enemies.

The greatness of Jacob is what is still sustaining the nation of Israel till today.

Chapter 8

JACOB AND RACHEL

JOSEPH

Jacob and Rachel were the third parents whom God called to fulfil the call of barrenness. And they happen to be the last parent to enjoy a successive transmission of the call from one generation to another. It was in their generation that the trans-generational transmission of the call of barrenness ceased. And wrong marriage was the cause of this abrupt cessation.

The story of the marriage of Jacob and Rachel has been briefly explained in the previous chapter.

Much has been said about Jacob in the previous chapters. In this chapter we would put the spotlight a little on Rachel and more on Joseph.

RACHEL

Rachel like all the other women with this call was barren. Rachel gave birth to two very important children Joseph and Benjamin. Joseph was the first child of Rachel. He became the kingly seed in his generation.

Genesis 30:22. And God remembered Rachel, and God hearkened to her, and opened her womb.
23. And she conceived, and bare a son; and said, God hath taken away my reproach:
24. And she called his name Joseph; and said, The LORD shall add to me another son.

Rachel was a very strong and hardworking woman. She was a shepherd girl, she was the one caring for her fathers sheep. She was like a man to the family.

Genesis 29:9. And while he yet spake with them, Rachel came with her father's sheep: for she kept them.

Rachel was very desperate to have children and in her desperation she began to look unto her husband Jacob for the fruit of the womb.

Genesis 30:1. And when Rachel saw that she bare Jacob no children, Rachel envied her sister; and said unto Jacob, Give me children, or else I die.
2. And Jacob's anger was kindled against Rachel: and he said, Am I in God's stead, who hath withheld from thee the fruit of the womb?

Rachel was a woman of deep conviction and passion for God, she was a woman that desired a passionate relationship with God, such that in her ignorance yet in a bid to have an intimate relationship with God, she stole her father's graven image until Jacob asked them to put away their strange gods and serve his own God.

Rachel was a woman of visions. It was such that she walked into the future and saw the time of the birth of Jesus. She saw the genocide killing of all the children in Bethlehem between the age of two years and under and wept bitterly for it. I would say she was a seer or a prophetess.

Matthew 2:17. Then was fulfilled that which was spoken by Jeremy the prophet, saying,
18. In Rama was there a voice heard, lamentation, and weeping, and great mourning, Rachel weeping for her children, and would not be comforted, because they are not.

Jeremiah 31:15. Thus saith the LORD; A voice was heard in Ramah, lamentation, and bitter weeping; Rahel weeping for her children refused to be comforted for her children, because they were not.
16. Thus saith the LORD; Refrain thy voice from weeping, and thine eyes from tears: for thy work shall be rewarded, saith the LORD; and they shall come again from the land of the enemy.

The trauma of this vision could be the reason she gave up the ghost during her child birth. Rachel experienced hard labour as they journeyed to Bethlehem and died while giving birth to her second son Benjamin (Genesis 35:16-19). It's possible that the vision she had on her way to Bethlehem (concerning the genocide killing that would happen there in the future) initiated the hard labour she had.

JOSEPH

Joseph was the third kingly seed to be brought into the world. Joseph was an exceptional young man. He was a man of vision. He was different from all the eleven sons of Israel; no wonder Jacob loved him more than all his brethren. I believe Jacob loved Joseph more than all his brethren because he possibly knew that Joseph was the called kingly seed, he possibly knew that upon Joseph lies the mantle for the continuity of the call of barrenness. No wonder when Joseph was presumed dead, he wept his heart out. He could not imagine that the kingly seed and only hope of sustaining the call would be gone just like that.

Genesis 37:3. Now Israel loved Joseph more than all his children, because he was the son of his old age: and he made him a coat of many colours.
4. And when his brethren saw that their father loved him more than all his brethren, they hated him, and could not speak peaceably unto him.
34. And Jacob rent his clothes, and put sackcloth upon his loins, and mourned for his son many days.
*35. And all his sons and all his daughters rose up to comfort him; but **he refused to be comforted;** and he said, For I will go down into the grave unto my son mourning. Thus his father wept for him.*

THE DREAMS AND VISIONS OF JOSEPH

The dreams of Joseph is a pointer to what has been ordained in the realm of the spirit concerning those with the call of barrenness. The revelations in Joseph's dreams is not peculiar to Joseph rather it applies to everyone with this call. In Joseph's dreams he often saw himself as a man of influence and authority. In his dreams he saw a future that God had destined for him.

Genesis 37:5. And Joseph dreamed a dream, and he told it his brethren: and they hated him yet the more.
6. And he said unto them, Hear, I pray you, this dream which I have dreamed:
*7. For, behold, **we were binding sheaves in the field, and, lo, my sheaf arose, and also stood upright; and, behold, your sheaves stood round about, and made obeisance to my sheaf.***
8. And his brethren said to him, Shalt thou indeed reign over us? or shalt thou indeed have dominion over us? And they hated him yet the more for his dreams, and for his words.
*9. And he dreamed yet another dream, and told it his brethren, and said, Behold, I have dreamed a dream more; and, **behold, the sun and the moon and the eleven stars made obeisance to me.***
10. And he told it to his father, and to his brethren: and his father rebuked him, and said unto him, What is this dream that thou hast dreamed? Shall I and thy mother and thy brethren indeed come to bow down ourselves to thee to the earth?
*11. And his brethren envied him; but **his father observed the saying.***

Joseph's dreams came to pass after many years of watching over the dreams. He became influential and powerful and became better than all the eleven sons of Jacob put together. Joseph was a living proof of the scripture that says whatsoever a blessed man does shall prosper.

*Genesis 39:2. And **the LORD was with Joseph, and he was a prosperous man**; and he was in the house of his master the Egyptian.*
*3. And **his master saw that the LORD was with him, and that the LORD made all that he did to prosper in his hand.***
4. And Joseph found grace in his sight, and he served him: and he made him overseer over his house, and all that he had he put into his hand.
5. And it came to pass from the time that he had made him overseer in his house, and over all that he had, that the LORD blessed the Egyptian's house for Joseph's sake; and the blessing of the LORD was upon all that he had in the house, and in the field.
6. And he left all that he had in Joseph's hand; and he knew not ought he had, save the bread which he did eat. And Joseph was a goodly person, and well favoured.

Joseph had an unusual grace and favour which I believe is common with all those with this call. Whatever Joseph touched became blessed and prospered because God was with him. Even when he was cast into prison, yet he became more prosperous in the prison. The location and situation of Joseph could not determine his prosperity, kingship and place in leadership. As a house boy (house keeper), he became the leader of the house, as a prisoner, he became the leader of prisoners. As a stranger in Egypt he became the leader and prime minister of Egypt. The leadership nature of the kingly seed kept manifesting in the life of Joseph wherever he found himself.

*Genesis 39:21. But **the LORD was with Joseph**, and shewed him mercy, **and gave him favour in the sight of the keeper of the prison.***
*22. And **the keeper of the prison committed to Joseph's hand all the prisoners that were in the prison;** and whatsoever they did there, he was the doer of it.*
*23. The keeper of the prison looked not to any thing that was under his hand; because the LORD was with him, and **that which he did, the LORD made it to prosper.***

The presence of God was always with Joseph and this I believe applies to all who have this calling. It didn't matter where Joseph was, the presence of God was there with him, whether in the pit, in prison, in a strange house, in a strange land, anywhere he was God was with him and showed him great favour.

Joseph had the spiritual gift of interpretation of dreams and he was always excited to share whatever he saw with anyone who cared to listen. This attitude of freely expressing his gift paved the way for the fulfilment of his dreams, vision and purpose. *His gift made room for him and brought him before great men.* This last statement just sparked a burst of inspiration about gifts right now in my spirit. Please permit me to drop it here for the benefit of those with this calling who may be born with one gift or the other.

GIFTS CREATE OPPORTUNITIES

Spiritual gifts when put to use create opportunities that never existed before. Your gift may not look relevant at the moment but by putting it to constant use, an opportunity, room or vacancy will be created for it. It may not look relevant at the moment but a problem or opportunity will be created that will make it relevant. The existence of a gift creates opportunities. That a gift exists means an opportunity or a place will soon be created for it. Gifts determine the opportunity or next area of relevance that will be created. The existence of a gift will always birth an opportunity for the manifestation and relevance of that gift. God creates opportunities in the direction of his gifting. God looks at the gifts that we put to use and creates an opportunity, room or area or relevance for it.

When Joseph started having dreams and interpreting them, it didn't look like a king would need it some day, but he kept putting it to use until it became like a job for him, he became known for it and BOOM an opportunity was created. God birthed the opportunity by putting a dream in Pharaohs head for the glory of Joseph knowing that only Joseph had the gift or ability to handle that opportunity at that time. Who could ever think that by just interpreting a dream one can become the prime minister of a nation? Your gift may not be conventional or popular but that's okay because that is what will single you out when an opportunity is created just for you by God. Dear reader, *"a man's gift makes room for him and bring him before great men"*. Your gift will give you your place at the top. Don't make light of your gifts.

Back to Joseph, he did not hesitate to use his gift of revelation even in the prison. He used it for both the poor and the rich. If he had despised using it on the poor, He would not have interpreted the dream of the king's servants. We must not hesitate to use our gifts at every opportunity. The dream the men had was an opportunity for Joseph to use his gift. I believe God made the two servants to have the dream they had in that one single night.

Genesis 40:5. And they dreamed a dream both of them, each man his dream in one night, each man according to the interpretation of his dream, the butler and the baker of the king of Egypt, which were bound in the prison.
6. And Joseph came in unto them in the morning, and looked upon them, and, behold, they were sad.
7. And he asked Pharaoh's officers that were with him in the ward of his lord's house, saying, Wherefore look ye so sadly to day?
*8. And they said unto him, **We have dreamed a dream, and there is no interpreter of it**. And Joseph said unto them, **Do not interpretations belong to God? tell me them, I pray you.***

Joseph used his gift of interpretation of dreams to serve both servants and masters alike. The service he rendered to Pharaoh's servants when the opportunity was created was what made him to meet Pharaoh. But note that, it took two full years after this opportunity, before God created the full blown opportunity that brought Joseph before Pharaoh, by making Pharaoh to dream. Below is the story from scriptures.

*Genesis 41:1. And it came to pass **at the end of two full years, that Pharaoh dreamed**: and, behold, he stood by the river.*

9. Then spake the chief butler unto Pharaoh, saying, I do remember my faults this day:

11. And we dreamed a dream in one night, I and he; we dreamed each man according to the interpretation of his dream.

13. And it came to pass, as he interpreted to us, so it was; me he restored unto mine office, and him he hanged.

*14. Then **Pharaoh sent and called Joseph, and they brought him hastily out of the dungeon**: and he shaved himself, and changed his raiment, and came in unto Pharaoh.*

*15. And Pharaoh said unto Joseph, **I have dreamed a dream, and there is none that can interpret it**: and I have heard say of thee, that thou canst understand a dream to interpret it.*

*16. And Joseph answered Pharaoh, saying, **It is not in me: God shall give Pharaoh an answer of peace.***

*25. And Joseph said unto Pharaoh, The dream of Pharaoh is one: **God hath shewed Pharaoh what he is about to do.***

28. This is the thing which I have spoken unto Pharaoh: What God is about to do he sheweth unto Pharaoh.

29. Behold, there come seven years of great plenty throughout all the land of Egypt:

30. And there shall arise after them seven years of famine; and all the plenty shall be forgotten in the land of Egypt; and the famine shall consume the land;

31. And the plenty shall not be known in the land by reason of that famine following; for it shall be very grievous.

*32. And for that **the dream was doubled unto Pharaoh twice; it is because the thing is established by God, and God will shortly bring it to pass.***

33. *Now therefore let Pharaoh look out a man discreet and wise, and set him over the land of Egypt.*

34. *Let Pharaoh do this, and let him appoint officers over the land, and take up the fifth part of the land of Egypt in the seven plenteous years.*

35. *And let them gather all the food of those good years that come, and lay up corn under the hand of Pharaoh, and let them keep food in the cities.*

36. *And that food shall be for store to the land against the seven years of famine, which shall be in the land of Egypt; that the land perish not through the famine.*

37. *And the thing was good in the eyes of Pharaoh, and in the eyes of all his servants.*

38. *And Pharaoh said unto his servants, **Can we find such a one as this is, a man in whom the Spirit of God is?***

39. *And Pharaoh said unto Joseph, **Forasmuch as God hath shewed thee all this, there is none so discreet and wise as thou art:***

40. *Thou shalt be over my house, and according unto thy word shall all my people be ruled: **only in the throne will I be greater than thou.***

41. *And Pharaoh said unto Joseph, **See, I have set thee over all the land of Egypt.***

42. *And Pharaoh took off his ring from his hand, and put it upon Joseph's hand, and arrayed him in vestures of fine linen, and put a gold chain about his neck;*

43. *And he made him to ride in the second chariot which he had; and they cried before him, Bow the knee: and he made him ruler over all the land of Egypt.*

44. *And Pharaoh said unto Joseph, I am Pharaoh, and without thee shall no man lift up his hand or foot in all the land of Egypt.*

God's will is to make His firstborn higher than the kings of the earth (Psalm 89:27), and this we see evident in the life of Joseph and all the others with this calling. Pharaoh said of Joseph, I have set you over the land of Egypt, including mine own house, by your word shall my people be ruled, only in the throne will I be greater than you (Genesis 41:40-41). In other words, the king was saying I give you the power to rule my people as you will but I will only keep the title of a king. I only keep the title but I give you the power. Pharaoh became a ceremonial king before Joseph; he only sat on the throne as king while Joseph became the ruler and king over the people.

Joseph was a man that feared God, he was a righteous man who would not sin against God no matter the temptation. We see from scriptures that even when he was repeatedly tempted and threatened by his master's wife he refused to commit sin. The fear of God in his heart withheld him from committing any evil.

Genesis 39:7. And it came to pass after these things, that his master's wife cast her eyes upon Joseph; and she said, Lie with me.
8. But he refused, and said unto his master's wife, Behold, my master wotteth not what is with me in the house, and he hath committed all that he hath to my hand;
9. There is none greater in this house than I; neither hath he kept back any thing from me but thee, because thou art his wife: **how then can I do this great wickedness, and sin against God?**
10. And it came to pass, as she spake to Joseph day by day,

that he hearkened not unto her, to lie by her, or to be with her.

Joseph was a man of impeccable reputation.

JOSEPH'S MARRIAGE TO ASENATH

Genesis 41:45. And Pharaoh called Joseph's name Zaphnath-paaneah; and he gave him to wife Asenath the daughter of Poti-pherah priest of On. And Joseph went out over all the land of Egypt.
46. And Joseph was thirty years old when he stood before Pharaoh king of Egypt. And Joseph went out from the presence of Pharaoh, and went throughout all the land of Egypt.

Asenath was the daughter of Potipherah the pagan priest. She was given as a wife to Joseph as a reward for interpreting Pharaoh's dream. This arrangement was a demonic ploy to corrupt Joseph's seeds which possibly was unknown to Joseph and even Pharaoh who was the human tool used. Joseph was the custodian of the kingly seed in his generation, however his marriage to Asenath, corrupted the kingly seed and caused it to cease for many generations.
God had warned the children of Israel not to marry tribes that serve other gods, the Egyptians were one of the forbidden tribes, that the children of Israel were warned not to marry. But here was Joseph marrying the daughter of the priest of the other gods, not just a commoner in the land but a daughter of the oracle of the Egyptian god. What happened here was not an ordinary event; it was influenced

by the devil. It was a demonic manipulation masterminded by the devil to corrupt God's kingly seed.

God's firstborn was shortchanged in this marriage between Joseph and Asenath, I strongly believe this was the reason behind God killing the firstborn sons of Egypt. God was avenging His firstborn son that was shortchanged. It's possible the devil had understood God's plan for the kingly seeds at that time and had seen that the only way to stop the continuity of the rise of this great kingly seeds in every generation is to corrupt the seed through an unholy marriage. In an unholy marriage a kingly seed is brought into a union with a corrupt womb thus corrupting the kingly seed. The devil knew how to corrupt the kingly seed, such that when the opportunity presented itself, he arranged his own daughter for Joseph to marry. The union between Joseph and Asenath was like light and darkness coming together in a union. It's like the devil giving his daughter to a child of God to marry. It was an unequal yoke, an unholy union. The devil after seeing Joseph's shinning star tried to get him to sin by using Potiphar's wife but Joseph stood strong and overcame. Its possible the devil since then had been strategizing and devising means to stop Joseph from fulfilling his calling. Remember the devil has always fought God's plan from the beginning. He took over Cain (the firstborn of humankind) in the Garden of Eden and is still seeking to take over God's firstborn sons. Cain was evil because he belonged to the Devil.

*1 John 3:12. Not as **Cain, who was of that wicked one**, and slew his brother. And wherefore slew he him? Because his own works were evil, and his brother's righteous.*

*Hebrews 11:28. Through faith he kept the passover, and the sprinkling of blood, lest **he that destroyed the firstborn should touch them.***

Note that all the people that God had warned the children of Israel not to marry are people that have been taken over by the Devil (Ezra 9:1-2). Note also that God had addressed Ephraim (the first son of Joseph by Asenath) as His firstborn (Jeremiah 31:9), but also note that because of the shortchange Ephraim clung to idols such that God had to let him alone (Hosea 4:17). Manasseh by birth was Joseph's firstborn son but by God's design according to the calling of barrenness, Ephraim was chosen to carry the mantle (Genesis 48:13-20). However by reason of the corruption of these seeds by Asenath's pagan foundation, they became attached to pagan idols and worship which of course are of the devil. Hence they were taken over by the devil. The corruption of Ephraim and Manasseh was majorly as a result of the corruption of the womb that bore them. Their glory departed right from the womb as a result of the corruption of their mother's womb (Hosea 9:11). We therefore see how that God's kingly seed was shortchanged.

God had to avenge His firstborn son that had been shortchanged by the devil in Egypt. God deliberately hardened the heart of Pharaoh so he could avenge His firstborn that had been shortchanged by killing the firstborn sons of Egypt at that time. Those firstborn sons of the Egyptians at that time were seen as children of the pagan gods, in other words children of the devil. It was more of a battle between the kingdom of God and the kingdom of the devil. It was a battle for the firstborn between these two kingdoms. God is very jealous for His firstborn sons who have the call of barrenness. Hence the vengeance that was meted on Pharaoh.

*Exodus 4:22. And thou shalt say unto Pharaoh, Thus saith the LORD, **Israel is my son, even my firstborn**:*
23. And I say unto thee, Let my son go, that he may serve me: and if thou refuse to let him go, behold, I will slay thy son, even thy firstborn.

Exodus 10:1. And the LORD said unto Moses, Go in unto Pharaoh: for I have hardened his heart, and the heart of his servants, that I might shew these my signs before him:

*Exodus 11:1. And the LORD said unto Moses, Yet will I bring one plague more upon Pharaoh, and upon Egypt; **afterwards he will let you go hence**: when he shall let you go, he shall surely thrust you out hence altogether.*
*5. And **all the firstborn in the land of Egypt shall die**, from the firstborn of Pharaoh that sitteth upon his throne, even unto the firstborn of the maidservant that is behind the mill; and all the firstborn of beasts.*

God could have made Pharaoh to let the children of Israel go free after the first plagues but God would not do that without avenging His firstborn son, God had to avenged His short-changed firstborn son before He made Pharaoh let His people go. When God killed the firstborns of Egypt, He sanctified to himself all the firstborns of Israel. God made a statement that day that will never be forgotten in the realm of the spirit and in the kingdom of darkness.

*Numbers 3:13. Because all the firstborn are mine; **for on the day that I smote all the firstborn in the land of Egypt I hallowed unto me all the firstborn in Israel,** both man and beast: mine shall they be: I am the LORD.*

We see in scriptures (Psalm 105:17-22) that most of the difficult and challenging situations Joseph went through before his glorification in Egypt was orchestrated by God to try him. But what I keep wondering about is how God would allow Joseph to marry Asenath, knowing that marrying her would corrupt the kingly seed. And I keep wondering, if Joseph had married another wife from his kin (since at that time a man could have more than one wife), could the kingly seed have found expression in the next generation? Did God bring Israel, Joseph's kin to Egypt so Joseph could get a wife from his kin to preserve the kingly seed? And was God expecting Joseph to make this move? If so, why did Joseph not see, know or understand it? Was this knowledge hid from Joseph or did Joseph's affluence and influence affect his perception and judgement? I believe God will provide the answer to these questions in your heart.

In the call of barrenness the peak of the fulfilment of the call is to transfer the call to the next generation. It is to produce a kingly seed. Not just a seed, a kingly seed. Joseph produced a seed, not a kingly seed. I see that the fulfilment of the call of barrenness does not completely depend on God. It depends on both God and the called. God has a part to play while the called also has a part to play. If God orchestrates things towards the fulfilment of the call and the called does not do what he is supposed to do, there is nothing God would do about it and the call will be interrupted at this point. This I believe was what happened with the interruption of the call in Joseph's time. The aspect where many with this call fail unknowingly is in the transference of the calling to the next generation perhaps because this knowledge was hid from them. Abraham, Isaac and Jacob successfully ensured the transfer of the call to the next generation but Joseph, Samuel, Samson and John did not sustain the continuity of the call.

Chapter 9

MANOAH AND WIFE

SAMSON

Manoah and his wife were the fourth couple called to fulfil the call of barrenness. After Jacob and Rachel it took **over** four hundred and seventy years before another couple (Manoah and his wife) were chosen to fulfil the call of barrenness. Yes! Over 470 years. Considering that the children of Israel were in bondage in Egypt for four hundred and thirty years and also considering that they spent forty years in the wilderness, just working with these two timelines, we can see that it took over 470 years for Samson the fourth kingly seed to be born.

*Exodus 12:40. Now the sojourning of the children of Israel, who dwelt in Egypt, was **four hundred and thirty years.***
*41. And it came to pass at the end of the **four hundred and thirty years**, even the selfsame day it came to pass, that all the hosts of the LORD went out from the land of Egypt.*

The error the sons of Jacob made in their choice of wives took over 470 years to fix. This is how costly disobedience to God's instruction is to man's destiny. What should have been a generational occurrence now took many generations (over 470 years) to manifest.

MANOAH AND WIFE

Judges 13:2. And there was a certain man of Zorah, of the family of the Danites, whose name was Manoah; and his wife was barren, and bare not.

Manoah was a descendant of Dan. Dan was Jacob's 5th son, and Bilhah's first child, which she bore to Jacob. Bilhah was Rachel's maid. Bilhah did not have a kingly womb so the union of her womb with Jacob's kingly seed could not produce the covenant seed at that time. However Dan retained a recessive kingly gene, which was passed through many generations to become dominant in Manoah, who was blessed to marry a woman with the kingly womb. The name of Manoah's wife was not clearly stated in the Bible. However, though nameless, yet her place and role in the birth of the fourth kingly seed gave her a name that was above whatever her real name was: the mother of Samson, the mother of the strongest man who ever lived.

Manoah's wife like all the other called women was barren. And like every other called woman, a time came to herald the arrival of the kingly seed and God sent an angel to announce the arrival of Samson to the mother.

She was made to understand the special nature of the child that was to be born; she was also given series of instructions that must be adhered to. Some of which include that the child Samson would be a Nazarite unto God from the womb, and as such the mother must not drink wine or strong drink nor eat any unclean thing while she is pregnant for the child. And when the child is born, his hair must not be cut or shaven.

*Judges 13:3. And the angel of the LORD appeared unto the woman, and said unto her, Behold now, thou art barren, and bearest not: but thou shalt conceive, and **bear a son**.*
*4. Now therefore beware, I pray thee, and **drink not wine nor strong drink, and eat not any unclean thing:***
*5. For, lo, **thou shalt conceive, and bear a son; and no rasor shall come on his head: for the child shall be a Nazarite unto God** from the womb: and **he shall begin to deliver Israel out of the hand of the Philistines.***

Manoah and his wife were a God fearing couple who were willing to do whatever God instructed them to do through his angel. They were people who were willing to receive and obey God's commandments to them through his servants. They believed the angel of God who initially they thought was a man of God and gladly received his message to them. They even went on to ask what else they must do to raise the child in the fear of the LORD.

Judges 13:12. And Manoah said, Now let thy words come to pass. How shall we order the child, and how shall we do unto him?

13. And the angel of the LORD said unto Manoah, Of all that I said unto the woman let her beware.
*14. She may not eat of any thing that cometh of the vine, neither let her drink wine or strong drink, nor eat any unclean thing: all that I **commanded** her let her observe.*

Manoah was also a man given to hospitality; he and his wife were hospitable to the angel who came to herald the coming of Samson. They were willing to honour the messenger whom God used to bring His word to them.
They offered to entertain the angel with food, but the angel declined the offer and asked that they offer it as a sacrifice unto God. And in offering the sacrifice unto God, the angel revealed himself to them.

Judges 13:15. And Manoah said unto the angel of the LORD, I pray thee, let us detain thee, until we shall have made ready a kid for thee.
16. And the angel of the LORD said unto Manoah, Though thou detain me, I will not eat of thy bread: and if thou wilt offer a burnt offering, thou must offer it unto the LORD. For Manoah knew not that he was an angel of the LORD.
17. And Manoah said unto the angel of the LORD, What is thy name, that when thy sayings come to pass we may do thee honour?

Judges 13:24. And the woman bare a son, and called his name Samson: and the child grew, and the LORD blessed him.
25. And the Spirit of the LORD began to move him at times in the camp of Dan between Zorah and Eshtaol.

After the annunciation of the arrival of the Nazarite by the angel, a male child was born to the couple and they called his name Samson, which means *"like the sun"*.

SAMSON

Samson was the fourth kingly seed to be born according to the biblical account of the kingly seed and of the call of barrenness. He was a Danite by decent. He was the kingly seed that came through the lineage of Dan, Jacob's fifth son.

Samson was the strongest man who ever lived and a judge of Israel for twenty years. He delivered God's people from 40 years of bondage under the Philistines.
Samson was a Nazarite from the womb. Nazarites are people who take a vow of separation or consecration unto God. They are described as being holy unto God. They vow to serve God all the days of their life, which is the ultimate will of God for all firstborns. This vow required that such a person abstain from all kinds of wine, that their hair must not be cut and they must not come in contact with corpse or dead bodies including those of their family members. Samson became the first kingly seed to be a Nazarite, after him the next two kingly seeds that followed Samuel and John the Baptist also became Nazarites from birth.

Samson's uncut hair locks became a source of supernatural strength to him. On his hair was hidden the secret of his strength and power, as such his hair was not meant to be cut. I see that the kingly seeds have to live under strict rules, observe God's principles and commandments if they must fulfil their calling as kingly seeds.

Samson's primary mission was to deliver the children of Israel from the hand of the Philistines. It seems that every kingly seed is born to fulfil a specific purpose. At this time the children of Israel were under the oppression of the Philistines and they needed to be liberated from their hand. Hence Samson was sent as a kingly seed in this generation to deliver the children of Israel.

Samson was a man of unusual strength and will. The Spirit of might found great expression in his life. Like we saw in the life of Joseph who had the gift of discernment and interpretation of dreams, Samson on the other hand had the gift of might or supernatural strength. At that time the children of Israel were under the captivity of the Philistines and the Philistines were known for their strength and resilience in battle. God had to raise a man at that time that has the strength and capacity to overcome the Philistines. Samson was so strong that at one instance he pulled the gate of a city along with its hinges and took them with him to the top of a hill, at another instance he killed a lion with his bare hands and at another instance he slew one thousand Philistines with the jawbone of an ass.

Judges 15:14. And when he came unto Lehi, the Philistines shouted against him: and the Spirit of the LORD came mightily upon him, and the cords that were upon his arms became as flax that was burnt with fire, and his bands loosed from off his hands.
15. And he found a new jawbone of an ass, and put forth his

hand, and took it, and slew a thousand men therewith.
16. And Samson said, With the jawbone of an ass, heaps upon heaps, with the jaw of an ass have I slain a thousand men.

The Philistines were not a match for Samson in strength and he did all he did by the Spirit of the LORD. Whenever the Spirit of the LORD came upon him, he manifested the supernatural strength of God.

The different giftings evident in the life of the kingly seeds point to the truth that it's important to discover the gifting of every kingly seed and harness it for the fulfilment of their purpose in life.

SAMSON AND WOMEN

Much of Samson's life was not documented in the Bible, except for his encounters with the women he loved. Samson was attracted to strange women who were not of his kin. First he was married to the philistine from Timnath, then he slept with the harlot at Gaza and then he fell in love with Delilah. Samson though loaded with the strength of the LORD, yet like every human he also needed love in his life. However, he sought for love in the wrong places, his choice of the woman Delilah became his undoing. Remember in this call, the woman you choose to marry plays a vital role in the fulfilment of the call. *(Please read Judges 16:1-30 for the full story of what transpired between Samson and Delilah).*

What we can learn from the life of Samson is that, like every human, these kingly seeds may have a fleshly weakness which if not properly handled can affect the fulfilment of the call. Jacob had his own weakness as we have seen earlier. Samson's weakness was women and to make things worse he was attracted to the wrong women. This points to the truth that those with this call must be careful in choosing their spouse because if they make the wrong choice it may not only affect their kingly seed but they themselves. From scriptures we can see that marrying the wrong woman can affect majorly two vital things in the life of the called seed. Firstly, it will corrupt the kingly gene, thus hindering the birth of a kingly seed or offspring. Secondly, it can cut short the life of the called seed thus hindering the fulfilment of the purpose of the called seed. Samson judged Israel for just twenty years unlike Samuel who judged Israel all the days of his life (1 Samuel 7:15). Possibly Samson was also meant to judge Israel all the days of his life like Samuel but this was cut short by his wrong choice of a woman.

From the life of Samson we can see that the gift of God in the life of the kingly seeds (that distinguishes them in their generation) can be lost if they get careless. Samson lost his strength, which came upon him as a result of the anointing of the Holy Spirit. This is a proof that the kingly seeds can lose their special gifting and anointing if they get disconnected from God. God left Samson the moment he broke the vow and Samson instantly lost his anointing (Judges 16:20). The loss of Samson's anointing made him a mockery and cost him his life. These kingly seeds must understand that they cannot do without God and to keep God in their affairs they must keep their part of the vow or covenant and obey every instruction of God to them. The kingly seeds must know or be made to know their part of the covenant and keep it. Their parents must know what God desires of them and teach it to them, raising them up in the fear of the LORD. The kingly seeds must allow God guide them in the choice of a wife. God did it for Isaac and Jacob; he can still do it for anyone.

Chapter 10

ELKANAH AND HANNAH

SAMUEL

Elkanah and his wife Hannah were the fifth couple that were called to fulfil the call of barrenness. The recessive kingly gene became dominant in their gene and found expression in their seed.

Elkanah had two wives Hannah and Penninah, Penninah was fertile but Hannah was barren. Though Hannah was barren yet Elkanah loved her more, just like Jacob loved Rachel who was barren more than Leah. I see that there is usually a soul tie between those who have this call, such that despite the barrenness yet the husband's love for the wife grows stronger. This I believe is the Creator's grand design to attract and keep the couple together for the fulfilment of the call.

Elkanah was a Levite by descent. In first Chronicles chapter six the lineage of Elkanah could be traced to the tribe of Levi. Elkanah though a Levite by decent, lived in mount Ephraim.

1 Samuel 1:1. Now there was a certain man of Ramathaim-zophim, of mount Ephraim, and his name was Elkanah, the son of Jeroham, the son of Elihu, the son of Tohu, the son of Zuph, an Ephrathite:
2. And he had two wives; the name of the one was Hannah, and the name of the other Peninnah: and Peninnah had children, but Hannah had no children.
3. And this man went up out of his city yearly to worship and to sacrifice unto the LORD of hosts in Shiloh. And the two sons of Eli, Hophni and Phinehas, the priests of the LORD, were there.
4. And when the time was that Elkanah offered, he gave to Peninnah his wife, and to all her sons and her daughters, portions:
5. But unto Hannah he gave a worthy portion; for he loved Hannah: but the LORD had shut up her womb.

Not much is written about Elkanah and Hannah, except that they always went to Shiloh yearly to pray, worship and sacrifice unto God. This shows that they were people who feared God and worshiped Him committedly.

As in the case of Sarah, Hannah's rival was also making her marriage unbearable for her. Peninnah was always taunting and provoking Hannah as a result of her barrenness. This is one major challenge the women with this call have to face, and this could come from either in-laws or family members. However, Hannah teaches us how to handle this kind of situations. Hannah transformed her sorrow and bitterness into a heartfelt prayer to God, weeping and pouring out her heart in sorrow unto God and God stepped in. One thing we must learn from the life of Hannah is how to channel our sorrows, bitterness and grievances to God in prayer.

1 Samuel 1:6. And her adversary also provoked her sore, for to make her fret, because the LORD had shut up her womb.
7. And as he did so year by year, when she went up to the house of the LORD, so she provoked her; therefore she wept, and did not eat.
8. Then said Elkanah her husband to her, Hannah, why weepest thou? and why eatest thou not? and why is thy heart grieved? am not I better to thee than ten sons?
9. So Hannah rose up after they had eaten in Shiloh, and after they had drunk. Now Eli the priest sat upon a seat by a post of the temple of the LORD.
10. And she was in bitterness of soul, and prayed unto the LORD, and wept sore.

Hannah prayed desperately to God such that Eli the priest thought she was drunk with wine. Hannah had to make a vow to God in the course of her prayer for the security of her unborn son. Hannah through her vow secured the child for God thus moving God to commit the child to her care. It's important to note that God does not just look at the vows made, he weighs every vow made before He commits the children to the custody of the parent.

*1 Samuel 1:11. And she vowed a vow, and said, O LORD of hosts, if thou wilt indeed look on the affliction of thine handmaid, and remember me, and not forget thine handmaid, but wilt give unto thine handmaid a man child, then **I will give him unto the LORD all the days of his life, and there shall no rasor come upon his head.***

12. And it came to pass, as she continued praying before the LORD, that Eli marked her mouth.

13. Now Hannah, she spake in her heart; only her lips moved, but her voice was not heard: therefore Eli thought she had been drunken.

14. And Eli said unto her, How long wilt thou be drunken? put away thy wine from thee.

15. And Hannah answered and said, No, my lord, I am a woman of a sorrowful spirit: I have drunk neither wine nor strong drink, but have poured out my soul before the LORD.

*19. And they rose up in the morning early, and worshipped before the LORD, and returned, and came to their house to Ramah: and **Elkanah knew Hannah his wife; and the LORD remembered her.***

*20. Wherefore it came to pass, when the time was come about after Hannah had conceived, that she bare a son, and **called his name Samuel**, saying, **Because I have asked him of the LORD.***

The call of barrenness is not an easy one, God does not just entrust this special kingly seeds to any parent; He screens the parents. He ensures that the parents (especially the mother) have in them the ability to bring the child up in the ways of the LORD and also ensures that the parent is willing to be committed and dedicated to putting this ability to work in the life of the child and not be like the man who was given one talent and refused to put his ability to work. It is written that to whom much is given much is also expected; God expects so much from these parents because a great destiny is being committed into their hands. These parents must therefore be willing to dedicate this special breed of children to God and keep them from being taken over by the devil, before they can be committed into their hands. The devil does not just sit there and watch these seeds grow and fulfil purpose, he fights them and hence God needs to ensure the parents are capable and committed to raising the child up in the ways of the LORD.

A practical example of this truth is seen in the life of the sons of Eli. Eli could not control or discipline his sons (1 Samuel 3:13), such that they became taken over by Belial, a demonic spirit. They were serving in the priest's office and committing all kinds of evil, causing the people of God to sin. They were even sleeping with women at the door of the tabernacle. What an abomination! They did so many abominable acts in God's temple, bringing the name of God to shame.

1 Samuel 2: 12. Now the sons of Eli were sons of Belial; they knew not the LORD.

God wants every parent to secure this special breed of men for Him, hence God would weigh their actions to see if they are equal to the task. These special children are not just put in the custody of any parent, their parents are **carefully chosen** by God.

From Hannah's prayer after the birth of Samuel I believe that Hannah got to understand the kingly status of the son that God has given to her.

1 Samuel 2:1. And Hannah prayed, and said, My heart rejoiceth in the LORD, mine horn is exalted in the LORD: my mouth is enlarged over mine enemies; because I rejoice in thy salvation.

5. They that were full have hired out themselves for bread; and they that were hungry ceased: so that the barren hath born seven; and she that hath many children is waxed feeble.

*10. The adversaries of the LORD shall be broken to pieces; out of heaven shall he thunder upon them: **the LORD** shall judge the ends of the earth; and he **shall give strength unto his king**, and exalt the horn of his anointed.*

The LORD shall give strength unto his king, and exalt the horn of his anointed. In the vocabulary of the spirit the horn represents the power, authority and dominion of a king. The visions of Daniel, John etc. reveals to us the mystery of a horn. Hannah in her prayer was speaking in the language of the spirit using spiritual vocabulary. Hannah knew that Samuel was not an ordinary child; she knew he was a spiritual king, a kingly priest and that was why she referred to him as a king. Remember she was speaking in the vocabulary of the spirit. I believe God opened her eyes of understanding to know the kind of child Samuel was, which of course guided her utterances in prayer. I believe through this book God will reveal to you many things about your unborn child thereby setting the stage for his arrival.

Interestingly, after Hannah gave birth to Samuel and dedicated him to God as she promised, she was given five more children as a compensation for Samuel according to the prayer of Eli the priest.

1 Samuel 2:20. And Eli blessed Elkanah and his wife, and said, The LORD give thee seed of this woman for the loan which is lent to the LORD. And they went unto their own home.

21. And the LORD visited Hannah, so that she conceived, and bare three sons and two daughters. And the child Samuel grew before the LORD.

God never leaves the barren, he keeps visiting them to perfect His plan and purpose for their life.

SAMUEL

Samuel was the fifth kingly seed to be born following biblical accounts. Samuel was a Levite by descent, that is, he was a descendant of the tribe of Levi, Jacob's third son. The kingly gene that was recessive in Levi became dominant in Elkanah, Samuel's father. In first Chronicles chapter six the lineage of Elkanah could be traced to the tribe of Levi. Looking at the genealogy of Samuel it took about ten generations from Jacob to Samuel. In other words it took about ten generations for the kingly gene to be purified and find expression. So for over ten generations there was no manifestation of the kingly seed because of the wrong choice in marriage by Jacob's children. However, looking at the actual years we see from the Holy Scriptures that it took about nine hundred and twenty years (920 years) after Joseph before Samuel the fifth kingly seed could be born.

*Exodus 12:40. Now the sojourning of the children of Israel, who dwelt in Egypt, was **four hundred and thirty years.***
*41. And it came to pass at the end of the **four hundred and thirty years**, even the selfsame day it came to pass, that all the hosts of the LORD went out from the land of Egypt.*

*Acts 13:18. And about the time of **forty years** suffered he their manners in the wilderness.*
19. And when he had destroyed seven nations in the land of Chanaan, he divided their land to them by lot.
*20. And after that he gave unto them judges about the space of **four hundred and fifty years, until Samuel the prophet.***

According to Moses, the children of Israel stayed in Egypt for 430 years and according to Paul's understanding and calculation it took about 490 after the exodus of the children of Israel from Egypt for Samuel to be born. Adding the years together as seen in the scriptures above, we have a total of 920 years. This is such a long time. The mistake of Levi in his choice of a wife took 920 years to correct. This is almost a millennium. A mistake that would take a millennium to fix is not a little mistake or one that can be easily overlooked. This is beyond a lifetime mistake; it is a millennial mistake. I believe you can now see why God was so angry with the children of Israel for their wrong choice of wives and why He warned them ahead of time.

SAMUEL THE SEER

Samuel was dedicated and separated unto God as a child and according to the covenant his mother made before his birth. As a child Samuel enjoyed the favour of the LORD, the kind we have noted in the life of Joseph (1 Samuel 2:26).

The LORD began to appear unto Samuel while he was a child. Samuel being a Seer by calling was able to communicate with God through visions as a child even when visions were rare in his time.

*1 Samuel 3:1. And the child Samuel ministered unto the LORD before Eli. And the word of the LORD was precious in those days; **there was no open vision.***
19. And Samuel grew, and the LORD was with him, and did let none of his words fall to the ground.
20. And all Israel from Dan even to Beer-sheba knew that Samuel was established to be a prophet of the LORD.
21. And the LORD appeared again in Shiloh: for the LORD revealed himself to Samuel in Shiloh by the word of the LORD.

Samuel was not just a judge and a prophet; he was also a kingmaker. He anointed Saul and David as kings in his lifetime, both of which depended on his counsel and guidance for their rulership.

Samuel like Jacob was a principality, he had the entire nation of Israel under his control. Through his intervention the children of Israel were delivered from the hand of the philistines and peace was restored in the territory and camp of the Israelites. Samuel was the last judge of Israel and he judged Israel all the days of his life.

1 Samuel 7:9. And Samuel took a sucking lamb, and offered it for a burnt offering wholly unto the LORD: and Samuel cried unto the LORD for Israel; and the LORD heard him.
10. And as Samuel was offering up the burnt offering, the Philistines drew near to battle against Israel: but the LORD thundered with a great thunder on that day upon the Philistines, and discomfited them; and they were smitten before Israel.

14. And the cities which the Philistines had taken from Israel were restored to Israel, from Ekron even unto Gath; and the coasts thereof did Israel deliver out of the hands of the Philistines. And there was peace between Israel and the Amorites.
15. And Samuel judged Israel all the days of his life.

Samuel died at a good old age and he had two sons who did not work in his footsteps. They did evil in the sight of God. Samuel did not produce a kingly seed after his kind. This possibly is because of the tribe of the woman he married though his wife's tribe was not mentioned in the bible.

1 Samuel 8:1. And it came to pass, when Samuel was old, that he made his sons judges over Israel.
2. Now the name of his firstborn was Joel; and the name of his second, Abiah: they were judges in Beer-sheba.
3. And his sons walked not in his ways, but turned aside after lucre, and took bribes, and perverted judgment.

It seem to me that, of all those with the call of barrenness in scriptures, only a few like Abraham, Isaac and Jacob were able to master the art of transference of the kingly seed from one generation to another. Except perhaps God destined it that they should not produce kingly seeds in their own time. Joseph, Samson, Samuel and John were the kingly seeds that did not have kingly offsprings to transfer the call of barrenness unto the next generation.

Chapter 11

ZACHARIAH AND ELIZABETH

JOHN

Zachariah and Elizabeth were the sixth couple with the call of barrenness. These couple were barren for a very long time; it was at a very old age that they fulfilled the call of barrenness. Both were righteous, blameless and God fearing. Zachariah was a priest while his wife Elizabeth was also of the lineage of priests.

*Luke 1:5. There was in the days of Herod, the king of Judaea, a certain priest named **Zacharias**, of the course of **Abia**: and his wife was of the daughters of **Aaron**, and her name was **Elisabeth**.*
6. And they were both righteous before God, walking in all the commandments and ordinances of the Lord blameless.
7. And they had no child, because that Elisabeth was barren, and they both were now well stricken in years.

Zachariah was a descendant of Judah, the fourth son of Israel (Jacob). He is said to be from Abia, Abia is the son of

Jeroboam, the son of Solomon. About thirty eight generations passed between the time of Judah to the time that John the Baptist was born, meaning it took about thirty eight generation for the kingly seed through Judah to become dominant and find expression. The precious kingly seed was undergoing genetic purification or purging within this period. It took this long possibly because of the woman Judah married.

*Matthew 1:17. So all the generations from Abraham to David are **fourteen generations**; and from David until the carrying away into Babylon are **fourteen generations**; and from the carrying away into Babylon unto Christ are **fourteen generations**.*

Adding together the generations from Abraham to Jesus (who was in the same generation with John) we have a total of forty-two generations. If we remove four generations from Abraham to Judah we have about thirty-eight generations before the arrival of John.

Elisabeth on the other hand was of the priestly lineage of Aaron, Moses blood brother. The mother of Moses and Aaron was Jochebed. Jochebed was the daughter of Levi, Jacob's third son from Leah. Note that the women from the lineage of Jacob through Leah and Rachel inherited the gene for the kingly womb, so the gene for the kingly womb was transferred from Leah and Rachel to their female children.

As it was with the other kingly seeds, when the time came for the womb of Elizabeth to be opened and for the kingly seed to be born, an angel was sent by God to herald the arrival of the kingly seed. Zachariah was discharging his priestly duties during a service when angel Gabriel appeared to him to announce the arrival of the special kingly seed. He was given conditions for raising the child and things that the child must not do. He was told that the child must not drink wine or alcoholic drink because he shall be filled with the Holy Spirit from the womb. This point to the truth that the Holy Spirit and alcohol cannot be mixed, in other words anyone who must be used by the Holy Spirit should not be given to alcohol.

Luke 1:8. And it came to pass, that while he executed the priest's office before God in the order of his course,
11. And there appeared unto him an angel of the Lord standing on the right side of the altar of incense.
12. And when Zacharias saw him, he was troubled, and fear fell upon him.
13. But the angel said unto him, Fear not, Zacharias: for thy prayer is heard; and thy wife Elisabeth shall bear thee a son, and thou shalt call his name John.
15. For he shall be great in the sight of the Lord, and shall drink neither wine nor strong drink; and he shall be filled with the Holy Ghost, even from his mother's womb.

The mission and purpose of the child was also given to Zachariah. Zachariah considering his age doubted the message of God to him through the angel and was made dumb as a sign that the word of God shall come to pass. Read below and see what followed thereafter.

Luke 1:16. And many of the children of Israel shall he turn to the Lord their God.

17. And he shall go before him in the spirit and power of Elias, to turn the hearts of the fathers to the children, and the disobedient to the wisdom of the just; to make ready a people prepared for the Lord.

18. And Zacharias said unto the angel, Whereby shall I know this? for I am an old man, and my wife well stricken in years.

19. And the angel answering said unto him, I am Gabriel, that stand in the presence of God; and am sent to speak unto thee, and to shew thee these glad tidings.

20. And, behold, thou shalt be dumb, and not able to speak, until the day that these things shall be performed, because thou believest not my words, which shall be fulfilled in their season.

24. And after those days his wife Elisabeth conceived, and hid herself five months, saying,

57. Now Elisabeth's full time came that she should be delivered; and she brought forth a son.

59. And it came to pass, that on the eighth day they came to circumcise the child; and they called him Zacharias, after the name of his father.

60. And his mother answered and said, Not so; but he shall be called John.

62. And they made signs to his father, how he would have him called.

63. And he asked for a writing table, and wrote, saying, His name is John. And they marvelled all.

64. And his mouth was opened immediately, and his tongue loosed, and he spake, and praised God.

66. And all they that heard them laid them up in their hearts, saying, What manner of child shall this be! And the hand of the Lord was with him.

THE PROPHESY OF ZACHARIAH

Zachariah being filled with the Holy Spirit after his mouth was opened (at the naming ceremony of John) prophesied concerning John the Baptist. I would say the Holy Spirit was speaking through him words concerning John. In this prophesy we see the Holy Spirit revealing the truth about the kingly seeds, how that John is a fulfilment of the covenant of the kingly seeds, which God made with Abraham many years ago.

*Luke 1:67. And his father **Zacharias was filled with the Holy Ghost, and prophesied, saying,***
68. Blessed be the Lord God of Israel; for he hath visited and redeemed his people,
69. And hath raised up an horn of salvation for us in the house of his servant David;
*70. As **he spake by the mouth of his holy prophets**, which have been since the world began:*
*72. **To perform the mercy promised to our fathers**, and **to remember his holy covenant;***
*73. **The oath which he sware to our father Abraham,***
*76. **And thou, child, shalt be called the prophet of the Highest: for thou shalt go before the face of the Lord to prepare his ways;***
77. To give knowledge of salvation unto his people by the remission of their sins,
80. And the child grew, and waxed strong in spirit, and was in the deserts till the day of his shewing unto Israel.

God had said to Abraham kings shall come out of thee while entering a covenant with Abraham and here we have the

Holy Spirit referring to John as a product of that covenant, thus validating the truth about the kingly seeds.

JOHN THE BAPTIST

John the Baptist was the sixth kingly seed and the last kingly seed documented in the holy Bible. John was a descendant of Judah, Jacob's fourth son. After the kingly gene through Judah was corrupted, it took about thirty-eight generations for the kingly gene to find expression in John.

Prophet Isaiah prophesied the coming of John to the earth many years before his arrival. I believe there are kingly seeds whose identities and missions are also revealed in scriptures. John was revealed in the scripture as, *"The voice of one crying in the wilderness, Make straight the way of the Lord."* He spent most of his life in the wilderness of Judaea eating locusts and wild honey as part of his daily diet. It's possible he escaped into the wilderness at a tender age during the Herodian genocide. In Luke's narrative it was written concerning John that, *"the child grew, and waxed strong in spirit, and was in the deserts till the day of his shewing unto Israel"* (Luke 1:80).

John lived a sacrificial life, a life without comfort, a life dedicated to the will of God, a life sacrificed for the salvation and reconciliation of mankind to God. John spent most of his life in the wilderness crying and praying for the reconciliation of men unto God. I can imagine his voice being heard from the wilderness daily for over twenty years of his youthful life, praying for the salvation of men and for the mercy of God upon mankind. He was in the wilderness until the time of his showing to Israel when the word of the LORD came to him, instructing him to come out of the wilderness and begin to baptise men (Luke 3:2-4).

John had one mission, which was to reveal Jesus Christ and to prepare the way for Him. Through the mystery of water baptism he revealed the identity of Jesus Christ and through the baptism of repentance, which he preached he prepared the heart of the people to receive Jesus. He was so committed to his mission that it became his identity, thus he was called John the Baptist. John the Baptist was the first man to ever baptise anyone in water and he was the first man to be given the assignment by God to baptise men.

John 1:31. And I knew him not: but that he should be made manifest to Israel, therefore am I come baptizing with water. 33. And I knew him not: but he that sent me to baptize with water, the same said unto me, Upon whom thou shalt see the Spirit descending, and remaining on him, the same is he which baptizeth with the Holy Ghost.

John knew his identity, his purpose and mission on the earth and he lived to fulfil it. John would say of himself "*I am the voice of one crying in the wilderness, Make straight the way of the Lord, as said the prophet Esaias.* All kingly seeds like John must know who they are and what their mission is on the earth.

John was the most influential man in his time. He was so influential that many thought he was the Christ that was to come and save the world. It was such that even priests and Levites came to him to inquire if he was the Christ. He was highly revered and respected by kings such that Herod feared him (Mark 6:20). The greatness of John the Baptist was approved and validated by the Lord Jesus Christ. The Lord Jesus said concerning John that, *"among them that are born of women, no one is greater than John the Baptist"*. (Matthew 11:11).

John was so great that he had to be removed out of the scene to prevent tension between his disciples and that of Jesus, because two great lights cannot shine at the same time. John's light was so bright until Jesus came into the scene. When Jesus came into the scene the light of John began to dim until it faded out of the scene. John understood this and would always say to his disciples, *"He must increase, but I must decrease"*.

John's relationship with Jesus was a close familial relationship, yet it seemed like they never had the opportunity to really interact as family. The only time John met Jesus after he came out of the wilderness was when Jesus came to be baptised by him. They pursued their calling to the detriment of their family relationship. This brings to mind the words of Jesus that a man who loves his family more than Him is not worthy of Him. This knowledge is important for all kingly seeds, as they must seek to please the one who has called them even at the expense of their own family. Jesus and John were cousins yet they never allowed familiarity to come in between them and their calling. John revered Jesus and saw himself as unworthy to lose the shoes of Jesus.

From scriptures we see that Elizabeth the mother of John and Mary the mother of Jesus were cousins. Their relationship was so close that when Mary came to visit the six months old pregnant Elizabeth, she had to stay with her for the third trimester of her pregnancy until John was born. When Mary came visiting John jumped in his mothers womb with excitement at the sound of Mary's voice. I can only imagine his excitement for the next three months that she stayed with them. John knew Jesus right from the womb; he honoured Jesus from the womb to the grave, from his first breath to his last breath, he was indeed a loyal servant to his Master. John lived a simple life, a Nazarite life, a separated life, a life consecrated unto God, a life dedicated to his purpose and mission on the earth. He lived a short but purpose full life.

Chapter 12

BARRENNESS AND RIGHT CHOICE OF SPOUSE

Many servants of God often feel that their wives cannot conceive because they got married to the wrong woman, that perhaps they are not destined to be together. However, looking at our fathers in the faith whose wives were barren, we would see that they were married to their God ordained spouses.

As a faithful servant of God, that your wife is barren is not a sign that you married the wrong person, rather it is a **proof** that you are married to your God ordained spouse. Rather than view barrenness as a consequence of your wrong choice in marriage, you should see that barrenness as a sign or validation that you are married to your God ordained spouse. As a faithful servant of God barrenness is actually a proof that God's hand is on your marriage, we see from scriptures that God's hand was what brought barrenness in the life of all who were barren in scriptures and whom God had interest in their wombs. The wombs that God had interest in were the only ones He closed or made barren. The fact that God shut up a womb is a proof that He is interested in that womb. That you are barren means God is highly interested in your womb.

God could not let Abimelech marry Sarah because her special kingly womb was not destined to carry his seed. Sarah's womb was destined to carry only Abraham's seed. Abraham's seed was destined to be carried by Sarah's womb to bring the promise of God to pass. To have Abimelech's seed in Sarah's womb would only breed a wrong combination. Note that when Abraham's seed was put in the wrong undestined womb of Hagar, the product became a thorn in the flesh of the promised seed, today that seed is what we see manifest as Islam.

That your wife is barren as a servant of God is a proof that you made the right choice in marriage. Remember how God led Abraham's servant to choose Rebecca for Isaac, we see that though she was chosen by God for Isaac yet she was barren. That your wife is barren even when it was God that led you to her is a proof that she is destined to bear your seed and a very special one at that. Here's the story of how God brought Rebecca to Abraham's servant.

Genesis 24:12. And he said, O LORD God of my master Abraham, I pray thee, send me good speed this day, and shew kindness unto my master Abraham.
13. Behold, I stand here by the well of water; and the daughters of the men of the city come out to draw water:
14. And let it come to pass, that the damsel to whom I shall say, Let down thy pitcher, I pray thee, that I may drink; and she shall say, Drink, and I will give thy camels drink also: let the same be she that thou hast appointed for thy servant Isaac; and thereby shall I know that thou hast shewed kindness unto my master.
15. And it came to pass, before he had done speaking, that,

behold, Rebekah came out, who was born to Bethuel, son of Milcah, the wife of Nahor, Abraham's brother, with her pitcher upon her shoulder.

16. And the damsel was very fair to look upon, a virgin, neither had any man known her: and she went down to the well, and filled her pitcher, and came up.

17. And the servant ran to meet her, and said, Let me, I pray thee, drink a little water of thy pitcher.

18. And she said, Drink, my lord: and she hasted, and let down her pitcher upon her hand, and gave him drink.

19. And when she had done giving him drink, she said, I will draw water for thy camels also, until they have done drinking.

20. And she hasted, and emptied her pitcher into the trough, and ran again unto the well to draw water, and drew for all his camels.

God is the one who calls men to fulfil the purpose of barrenness and because this calling is highly dependent on marriage, God becomes the matchmaker. God matched Isaac with Rebecca; He is still in the business of matching couples for the purpose of this calling. I hear preachers say, since Adam blamed his fall on the woman God gave him, God stopped matchmaking people. Can I tell you the truth? That is an erroneous statement made out of ignorance and lack of understanding of the truth. If what they say is true why then did God match Isaac and Rebecca? And many others that we see and hear about even today? Don't be deceived God is still in the business of matchmaking couples especially for the purpose of the call of barrenness. You must therefore depend on Him in your quest for your God ordained spouse.

Chapter 13

HOW TO LIVE TO FULFIL THE CALLING

In this chapter, we look at how to live in your season of unfruitfulness/waiting in other to secure God's attention.

1. Be joyful and rejoice.

Galatians 4:27. For it is written, Rejoice, thou barren that bearest not; break forth and cry, thou that travailest not: for the desolate hath many more children than she which hath an husband.

Let your barrenness make you rejoice, let the expectation of the child that would be born out of your barrenness make you joyful. Think about the greatness of that seed that would be born after your season of barrenness is over and let that thought make your heart leap for joy.

2. Sing and Praise God despite the barrenness.

Isaiah 54:1. Sing, O barren, thou that didst not bear; break forth into singing, and cry aloud, thou that didst not travail with child: for more are the children of the desolate than the children of the married wife, saith the LORD.
13. And all thy children shall be taught of the LORD; and

great shall be the peace of thy children.
Sing! One thing the barren are encouraged to do is to sing. Channel all your emotions into singing a joyful song unto the LORD. Express your joy unto the LORD for choosing you to fulfil this special calling by singing.

3. Be righteous.

Every divine calling is sustained by righteousness. From Abraham unto Zachariah, we see that they were all righteous people. Concerning the barren, it is written, *"in righteousness shalt thou be established"*.

Isaiah 54:14. In righteousness shalt thou be established: thou shalt be far from oppression; for thou shalt not fear: and from terror; for it shall not come near thee.

4. Understand that God has a reason for your barrenness.

Understand that the One who created you and made you barren knows what He is doing. Understand that He has a purpose for that barrenness.
Hear what God is saying to you today.

Isaiah 29:16. Surely your turning of things upside down shall be esteemed as the potter's clay: for shall the work say of him that made it, He made me not? or shall the thing framed say of him that framed it, He had no understanding?
17. Is it not yet a very little while, and Lebanon shall be turned into a fruitful field, and the fruitful field shall be esteemed as a forest?

18. And in that day shall the deaf hear the words of the book, and the eyes of the blind shall see out of obscurity, and out of darkness.
19. The meek also shall increase their joy in the LORD, and the poor among men shall rejoice in the Holy One of Israel.
22. Therefore thus saith the LORD, who redeemed Abraham, concerning the house of Jacob, Jacob shall not now be ashamed, neither shall his face now wax pale.
23. But when he seeth his children, the work of mine hands, in the midst of him, they shall sanctify my name, and sanctify the Holy One of Jacob, and shall fear the God of Israel.
24. They also that erred in spirit shall come to understanding, and they that murmured shall learn doctrine.

Accept your barrenness with meekness and let God bring His will to pass in your life.

5. Seek to hear God.

Stop assuming things; stop assuming what God wants for you. Rather seek to know what He is saying concerning your barrenness. Our ways are not God's ways, neither are our thoughts His thoughts, therefore never think for God or assume God's plan for you. Assumption they say is the mother of all mistakes and failures. Many times we fail to receive God's blessings because we think for God. All the once barren women as we have seen, sought God desperately and most of them had personal revelations about God's plan for them and their children.
Ask God to reveal His plan for you. We can discover God's plan for our life by praying and studying the word of God.

6. Fear God.

Psalm 128:1. Blessed is every one that feareth the LORD; that walketh in his ways.
*3. **Thy wife shall be as a fruitful vine** by the sides of thine house: thy children like olive plants round about thy table.*
4. Behold, that thus shall the man be blessed that feareth the LORD.
6. Yea, thou shalt see thy children's children, and peace upon Israel.

The fear of God secures the blessings of God. The fear of God makes barren women fruitful. The fear of God will keep you righteous and in tune with God. All the aforementioned couple with this call were all God fearing people. Everyone with this calling must also strive to be God fearing.

7. Be patient with God.

Hebrews 10:36. For ye have need of patience, that, after ye have done the will of God, ye might receive the promise.
37. For yet a little while, and he that shall come will come, and will not tarry.

One very important virtue required for this calling is patience. Waiting for the promised seed demands patience. Even after doing the will of God, you need to patiently wait to receive the promise. After the promise was given to Abraham, it took 25 years before Isaac was born. After Isaac married Rebecca it took them 20 years before Rebecca could conceive.

Fulfilling the call of barrenness demands patience. Your barren years are your waiting years, you must therefore patiently wait for your fruitful years, for *"It is good that a man should both hope and quietly wait for the salvation of the LORD"* (Lamentations 3:26).

8. Pray and ask God to open your womb.

The need to seek God's face in prayer on this matter cannot be overemphasised. We see that God in His infinite wisdom withheld children from Isaac and Rebecca until Isaac prayed earnestly for his wife. Praying to God serves as a reminder to God.

Genesis 25:21. And Isaac intreated the LORD for his wife, because she was barren: and the LORD was intreated of him, and Rebekah his wife conceived.

This special breed of children who come through the barren wombs could only come in a spiritual way, and hence must be sought for in prayer. Please note that you must pray to God yourself as a husband or as a wife. This is not what you meet a prophet to pray for you, or contract a pastor or someone to pray for you, it is what you must do for yourself. A prophet can however use his prophetic office to amplify your own prayers to bring your desire to pass. Note that when Eli the prophet met Hannah in first Samuel one seventeen he said to her **"Go in peace: and the God of Israel grant thee thy petition that thou hast asked of him".** And Hannah conceived after that. Eli used his prophetic office to amplify Hannah's prayer. Without your prayers a prophet will not have a prayer to amplify.

Note however, that you can pray for many years and still not conceive. That does not mean that your prayers have not been heard. Therefore do not get discouraged, if after many years of prayers nothing happens. Just know that God is preparing you for what is coming. He is working behind the scene.

9. Don't be afraid.

In God's message to the barren, He made it clear that the barren must not fear, because God will not allow them to be put to shame. Don't be afraid of what people would say because God will shut the mouth of those same people.

Isaiah 54:4. ***Fear not; for thou shalt not be ashamed:*** *neither be thou confounded; for thou shalt not be put to shame: for thou shalt forget the shame of thy youth, and shalt not remember the reproach of thy widowhood any more.*
5. For thy Maker is thine husband; the LORD of hosts is his name; and thy Redeemer the Holy One of Israel; The God of the whole earth shall he be called.
*6. **For the LORD hath called thee as a woman forsaken and grieved in spirit, and a wife of youth**, when thou wast refused, saith thy God.*
7. For a small moment have I forsaken thee; but with great mercies will I gather thee.

God has said everything you are experiencing is as a result of your calling. It is what He himself has called you to experience therefore there is no need to fear about the uncertainties of the future because a fruitful future is guaranteed for you. Every barren woman is privileged to have God as her husband. Every good husband would want his wife to conceive and bear children. Having the Good LORD as your husband therefore guarantees your fruitfulness.

10. Trust God and believe His word.

Luke 1:6. And they were both righteous before God, walking in all the commandments and ordinances of the Lord blameless.
7. And they had no child, because that Elisabeth was barren, and they both were now well stricken in years.
11. And there appeared unto him an angel of the Lord standing on the right side of the altar of incense.
13. But the angel said unto him, Fear not, Zacharias: for thy prayer is heard; and thy wife Elisabeth shall bear thee a son, and thou shalt call his name John.
45. And blessed is she that believed: for there shall be a performance of those things which were told her from the Lord.

Elizabeth the mother of John the Baptist was barren and when God wanted to change her story, He sent an angel with a message to her husband that she will bear a son. Note that God did not speak to Elizabeth directly, He sent an angel who spoke to her husband, who in turn passed the information to her, in other words she had third hand message or information from God. The message of fruitfulness came to her from God through an angel and through her husband. By the time the message got to her it became third hand message. Nevertheless, Elizabeth believed everything that God sent His messenger to tell her and it came to pass as spoken by the mouth of the messenger. God performed what He sent His angelic messenger to tell her. God is still sending His messengers to men today and these messengers could come as Angels and as men.

11. Eliminate anxiety

Anxiety means to be uneasy, troubled or eager about something. Instead of being anxious, we are encouraged to rather pray and thank God.

Philippians 4:6. Be careful for nothing; but in every thing by prayer and supplication with thanksgiving let your requests be made known unto God.

Let's see the same scripture from another bible translation, the New International Version.

Philippians 4:6 (NIV). Do not be anxious about anything, but in every situation, by prayer and petition, with thanksgiving, present your requests to God.

When you carefully monitor your ovulation date before you meet with your spouse you are being anxious. Don't go about carefully calculating your ovulation date and carefully timing yourself to conceive. Don't bother yourself with your fertile period in accordance with science because when God shuts a womb there is nothing science can do to open it. If God is the one who shut a womb, you can try all scientifically proven methods for conception and still not conceive.

Don't be anxious at all. Commit all into God's hands through prayer and give Him thanks for creating you the way you are. Stop timing your conception, let God do the timing. God knows the perfect timing for the conception of His covenant seed. Science says there is a specific timing of ovulation that determines the conception of a male or female seed but have you noticed that all the first seed of the called barren women are all males? None mistakenly came out as female. That is because God has a perfect timing for the conception of the covenant seed. God's timing for the conception of the covenant seed does not depend on proven scientific methods and that is why as a woman with a called womb, you don't have to be anxious about the conception of the seed. Know that God is in control of the conception of the covenant seed. When you know this, you will not be anxious and your heart will be at peace.

I believe that by reason of what you have seen in this book, you will have no reason to be anxious about being pregnant, because God is in control. Let God be in control and you will have nothing to worry about.

12. Keep serving God faithfully

*Exodus 23:25. And **ye shall serve the LORD your God**, and he shall bless thy bread, and thy water; and I will take sickness away from the midst of thee.*
*26. There shall nothing cast their young, **nor be barren, in thy land**: the number of thy days I will fulfil.*

Serving God faithfully guarantees fruitfulness. We see clearly in the life of Elkanah and Zachariah that it was at their point of service unto God that they were visited.

The fruit of the womb is one of God's rewards for serving Him. For those whose barrenness is as a result of their sin or any other cause beside the barrenness of purpose, serving God faithfully attracts a reward of the fruit of the womb. Serving God in truth and in spirit can make you fruitful. The scriptures below will help our faith.

Psalm 127:3. Lo, children are an heritage of the LORD: and the fruit of the womb is his reward.

1 Peter 3:12. For the eyes of the Lord are over the righteous, and his ears are open unto their prayers: but the face of the Lord is against them that do evil.
13. And who is he that will harm you, if ye be followers of that which is good?

God still rewards His faithful servants with the fruit of the womb.

13. Stay planted in God's house

Psalm 92:13. Those that be planted in the house of the LORD shall flourish in the courts of our God.
*14. **They shall still bring forth fruit in old age**; they shall be fat and flourishing;*
15. To shew that the LORD is upright: he is my rock, and there is no unrighteousness in him.

We must stay planted in God's house to enjoy and experience His presence. Those that are planted in God's house are the only ones that bring forth fruit in their old age. They are the ones that menopause has no power over. For us to bear fruits even in old age, we must get planted in God's house and take root downwards. We must never go to seek help from other gods, from native doctors, diviners etc.

Psalm 16:4. Their sorrows shall be multiplied that hasten after another god: their drink offerings of blood will I not offer, nor take up their names into my lips.
11. Thou wilt shew me the path of life: in thy presence is fulness of joy; at thy right hand there are pleasures for evermore.

Those who leave the house of God or the church of God to seek help or fruitfulness from other gods, native doctors, demonic prayer houses etc. shall have their sorrows multiplied, so it is not an option. If you go after other gods God will not mention your name to the Angels to deliver your blessing of the fruit of the womb when it's time for you to receive the blessing.

No one suffers shame and reproach being planted in God's house for in God's presence there is fullness of joy and pleasures forever. In the presence of God lies the solution to man's problems for *"Upon mount Zion shall be deliverance, and there shall be holiness; and the house of Jacob shall possess their possessions (Obadiah 1:17)."* Mount Zion is the house of God or church of God and we possess our possessions of children by being planted in Mount Zion.

CONCLUSION

Barrenness is a natural camouflage over a supernatural agenda. Barrenness is a veil. And after the veil lies the glory. We must therefore look beyond the veil to see the glory behind barrenness. This book reveals the glory behind the veil of barrenness.

Barrenness among God's faithful servants is not a curse but a blessing in disguise. If found amongst God's faithful servants barrenness can serve as a harbinger of the miraculous birth of a divinely chosen spiritual male leader. We have seen that the sons born to the once barren women in scriptures were singled out as special and unique in their generations. Barrenness marks a child for divinely ordained spiritual leadership. Barrenness among God's faithful servants is not a curse but a mark of a womb chosen by God to bear a very special breed of children.

It seems to me that some of the kingly seeds did not have a grasp of the great plan and purpose God had for them. But for you reading this book, I believe looking through their life and learning from them, you now know better what they did not know. Now that you know and understand the truth, you will be able to run the race without stumbling.

Beloved in Christ, this revelation is written for your blessing, that as you read, you may run with it and fulfil the glorious purpose for which you have been called. That as a parent you will be able to guide your kingly seed and as a kingly seed you will be able to run with God's plan and purpose for your life.

I can tell you with all certainty that many kingly seeds will be born in these last days, for they shall be God's battle axe and weapons of war against the enemies of God's kingdom. Therefore if you are reading this and you are barren, I like you to get excited because I can tell you assuredly that God is looking in your direction, He is looking to open the womb of those He has specially created to fulfil the purpose of bringing forth the precious and special kingly seeds.

If you have read this book to this point, I believe it has been a wonderful journey of divine revelations for you. I believe the Holy Spirit would have spoken to you as you journeyed through the pages of this book. I believe your heart is full of joy, your faith is stirred up and you have received strength to run with the vision of your calling.

For you who has reached menopause, with rapturous joy in my heart I CONGRATULATE you and I WELCOME you to your FRUITFUL season. CONGRATULATION!

For me, it has been a wonderful journey writing this book. It was a one-year journey of revelations, Holy Spirit brooding, guidance and purposeful transcription of divinely inspired insights and revelations. I thank the Almighty God and Creator of all things, my Maker, your Maker, for giving me this message to you. I thank God for choosing me as a medium to reveal this great mystery to all who are called to fulfil the ministry of barrenness.

My earnest prayer for you is that you will fulfil your calling both as a called parent and as a kingly seed.

I look forward to hear your testimonies.

God bless you.

Please keep in touch.
We would love to hear from you.

Kindly send us the testimonies of your encounter with this book to the email
contactogan@gmail.com

Follow my pages on Facebook:
@PstChristopherOgan
@TheLivingWordDevotional
WhatsApp: +2348109670769

To support this work of God:

Please PayPal me on **paypal.me/ChrisOgan**

If in Nigeria, please use the account below.
    Name: Christopher Ogan
    A/c No: 0701295026
    Bank: Access Bank

OTHER BOOKS BY THE AUTHOR

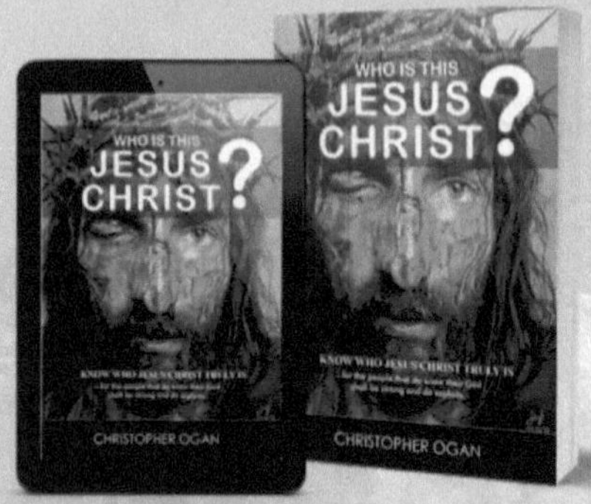

Please get
copies of
this books
on

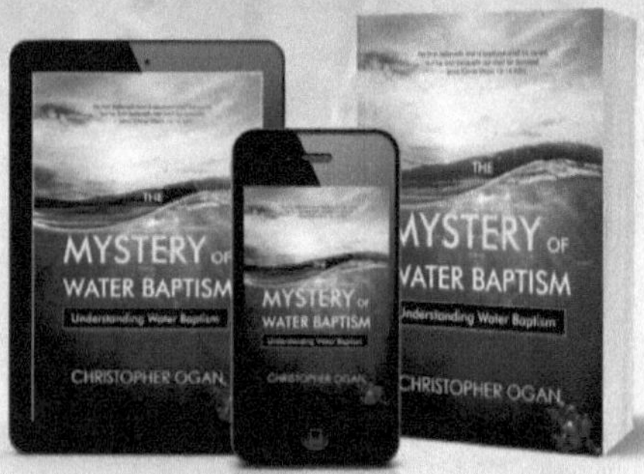

*Through this books
you will...*

Get to know
Jesus Christ better

Understand
Water Baptism

&

Be Truly
Born Again